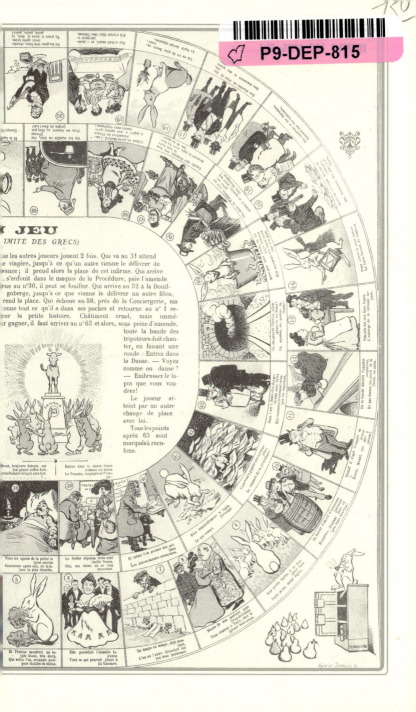

# La Grande
# Thérèse

ALSO BY HILARY SPURLING

*The Unknown Matisse:*
*A Life of Henri Matisse, The Early Years,*
*1869–1908*

*Ivy: The Life of Ivy Compton-Burnett*

*Paul Scott: A Life*

*Elinor Fettiplace's Receipt Book*

Thérèse Humbert's best friend, Catherine Parayre, at the Humbert weddings in Beauzelle in 1878, with her husband and their six-year-old daughter, Amelie, who grew up to marry the painter Henri Matisse.
*(Collection of Gaetana Matisse)*

# La Grande Thérèse

## The Greatest Scandal
## of the Century

## Hilary Spurling

HarperCollins*Publishers*

Every effort has been made to contact all copyright holders of the illustrations. The publishers will be glad to correct any errors or omissions brought to their attention.

HarperCollins books may be purchased for educational, business, or sales promotional use. For information please write: Special Markets Department, HarperCollins Publishers Inc., 10 East 53rd Street, New York, NY 10022.

Originally published in the United Kingdom in 1999 by Profile Books Ltd.

First American edition published in 2000.

*Designed by Nancy B. Field*

*Picture research by Gráinne Kelly*

Printed on acid-free paper

**Library of Congress Cataloging-in-Publication Data**

Spurling, Hilary.
   La Grande Thérèse : the greatest scandal of the century / Hilary Spurling—1st ed.
      p. cm.
   ISBN 0-06-019622-X
   1. Humbert, Thérèse, b. 1856.   2. Impostors and imposture—France—Biography.   3. France—Biography.   I. Title.
CT9981'2'092—dc21
   [B]                                                        99–462221

00 01 02 03 04  ❖/RRD 10 9 8 7 6 5 4 3 2 1

# Illustrations

## Illustrations

# Illustrations

Thérèse Daurignac was born in 1856 in the far southwest of France, in the province called Languedoc, once celebrated for its troubadours and their romances. Life for Thérèse in the little village of Aussonne, just outside Toulouse, was anything but romantic. She was the eldest child in a poor family: a stocky, bright-eyed little girl, not particularly good-looking, with nothing special about her except the power of her imagination. Thérèse told stories. In an age without television, in a countryside where most people still could not read, she transformed the narrow, drab, familiar world of the village children into something rich and strange. From their earliest years she entertained her five siblings with tales in which their father became the Comte d'Aurignac, Thérèse herself stood to inherit a fortune, and the family's modest farmhouse turned into a château.

Every house Thérèse ever inhabited became a château in her mind's eye. The first of her pure inventions was the Château de Marcotte, which stood on gleaming marble pavements among flower gardens and walks lined with orange trees on shady slopes above the sea where the Pyrenees mark the border between France and Spain. It was as far as a child's imagination could reach from the hot, dusty inland plain around Aussonne. A trip to the mountains fifty miles to the west, or to the Mediterranean coast nearly a hundred miles to the south, would have taken many days by cart or horseback along the stony tracks of Languedoc. For peasant children growing up in the flat, featureless fields behind Toulouse, Marcotte and its castle by the sea might as well have been in fairyland.

When Thérèse was small, she invented palaces for her siblings to live in, and once she was grown up, her castles in the air came true. In her prime she moved her whole family into a stately mansion with

*Landscape, Toulouse*, 1899, pen-and-ink drawing by Henri
Matisse, who married the daughter of Thérèse's best friend
and spent part of his honeymoon sketching and painting
the flat fields around Aussonne. *(Private collection;
© H. Matisse/DACS London, 1999; photo: Archives Matisse,
Paris; all rights reserved)*

marble halls full of fine paintings and gilt furniture
in the wealthiest part of Paris. They spent summers
in one or another of her country houses, each surrounded by its own parkland and hunting grounds

or vineyards. La Grande Thérèse, as she was called, remained for twenty years one of the most conspicuous and powerful women in France. Parisian high society vied for her favors. It was a fairy-tale outcome for an uneducated village girl born at the bottom of the social heap, with her imagination as her only capital.

Thérèse's parents were bastards. Her father had been a foundling, discovered as a baby in a church tower in Toulouse and promptly turned over to the local orphanage. Nameless babies born out of wedlock in the back streets or outlying villages of a city like Toulouse had no civil rights, no papers, and no prospects. The boy, Guillaume Auguste, belonged to nobody, and made up for it by hanging around the church, which was the only home he knew. He was finally taken in by the parish priest (generally supposed to be his natural father), who taught him to serve mass, made the most of his strong singing voice, and encouraged his taste for dressing up by putting him in charge of church vestments. Auguste went on to become for fifteen years a bishop's valet.

He acquired an identity of his own for the

first time at the age of thirty-eight, when a respectable Toulouse matron, the widow Doyen, officially claimed him as her son, giving him her maiden name, Daurignac. She had been comfortably provided for by her late husband, who was a clock- and watchmaker, but the new Auguste Daurignac welcomed this long-lost mother without enthusiasm. He had provided himself with a rather more romantic ancestry in the private dreamworld into which he could retreat as if by magic. The local people recognized him as a visionary, someone out of the ordinary, part simpleton, part sorcerer, to be treated warily for fear he would make mischief or cast spells. He was a courtly figure, frock-coated, top-hatted, at once formal and flamboyant: something of a catch when, in 1852 at the age of fifty-one, he finally married Lucie Rosa Capella, who was half his age.

Rosa was herself the illegitimate daughter of a rich farmer called Duluc. A wily operator with a reputation as both a libertine and a skinflint, old Father Duluc was famous for having gotten the better of a highwayman who held him up on the way home from market. Far from making off with the farmer's bags of gold, the would-be mugger was forced to accept a check instead, only to find the police waiting for him when he called at the bank to cash it. Rosa's mother was Madame Capella, the wife of another valet. Duluc, who never married, fathered many offspring, all of whom grew up hoping to come into his substantial fortune. In the end he left everything to his favorite of Madame Capella's three daughters, a young Madame Dupuy, who celebrated her good luck by presenting each of her sisters with a dowry of one thousand francs.

Rosa Daurignac invested her money in a farmhouse called L'Oeillet at Aussonne, where her husband proposed to earn a living as a freelance bone setter, marriage broker, and faith healer. The country people of Languedoc still lived by the seasonal rhythms, rituals, and superstitions of the Middle Ages, virtually untouched as yet by the new world of industrial expansion already beginning to transform ancient cities like Toulouse.

The Daurignacs stood out in the village. Not exactly landowners, they did not fit easily into the community of laborers, smallholders, and tenant farmers who scraped a meager living from the soil. A girl and two boys were born in quick succession: Thérèse, Emile, and Romain Daurignac. Their father solved the family's social problem by taking on a new role—a part he felt himself born to play—as unofficial lord of the manor.

But the peasants who were his clients paid little or nothing. Debts mounted, and the Daurignacs' income remained at best sporadic. Rosa, who was not her father's daughter for nothing, took out a mortgage on her house, moved into town with her little daughter, and opened a boutique selling high-class lingerie to the wives of wealthy industrialists on one of the smartest shopping streets in Toulouse. The business grew in the 1860s, and so did the family. Another boy, Louis, was followed by two more girls: Marie-Louise and Maria. The Daurignacs might have prospered if their mother had not died prematurely at L'Oeillet in January 1871, leaving her small children and their elderly father with no money coming in and no one to look after them but the fourteen-year-old Thérèse.

Over the next few years the family's situation

Thérèse Humbert · Frédéric Humbert · Maria Daurignac

Nous sommes passés par ici
Nous repasserons par là
Mais sur l'honneur, hors Paris
De vrates poir's ne poussent pas *(bis)*

C'est la fille vingt fois fiancée,
Dont les fleurs sont restées... rosiers!
Battez donc, ô *Mesrs* du sport,
Cet unique et... sublime record.

Mlle Ève HUMBERT

Thérèse's childhood dreams come true: Thérèse, pictured at the height of her fame as a society hostess in Paris, with her husband, Frédéric Humbert; her only daughter, Eve; and her younger sister, Maria Daurignac. *(Photo: © Topham Picturepoint)*

went from bad to worse. Auguste Daurignac withdrew into himself, sunk in fantasy, ignoring creditors or fending them off with talk of unspecified legal documents in a locked chest and, failing that, with the threat of magic powers. He pored over a seventeenth-century recipe book, said to be a work of alchemy containing instructions for wreaking havoc on his neighbors or, alternatively, granting their hearts' desire. He told fortunes, prophesied good or bad harvests, hinted at possession of a mighty secret. The villagers, who had accepted Daurignac's eccentricities as relatively harmless in his wife's lifetime, now looked on him uneasily as a necromancer. People remembered him in his seventies running across the fields, wild-eyed and waving a wand, in thunderstorms he claimed to have conjured up himself. Many assumed he was the children's grandfather. "He was a great booby, a good-for-nothing, he had *no* control over his children," said a barber called Bérard, who first came across the Daurignacs just before their mother's death, when things began to go wrong for them. "The head of the family was Thérèse."

Old Father Daurignac could still extract an occasional offering—a pat of butter, a basket of eggs, perhaps a chicken or a brace of game—from poor farmers who half believed in his ability to blight their crops by calling down rain or hailstones. But it was left to Thérèse to beg, borrow, and scrounge the family's daily living. Emile and

Romain followed her lead. "She was a bright little thing in those days," said Bérard: "very talkative, already—after her mother died—running the whole outfit." Thérèse fed the children, mothered the baby, and kept everybody's spirits up with her tall stories. Friends and neighbors were touched by her buoyancy and courage. Bérard was one of her earliest admirers. Another was the curé, Abbé Piette, whose support counted for much in Aussonne. A third was the bailiff's daughter, Catherine Fuzié, a dark-eyed beauty with the air of hauteur and reserve that traditionally conceals deep feeling among the women of her native South.

Catherine's fierce protective instincts responded unconditionally to Thérèse, who was eight years younger. The two had known one another as long as either could remember. "I practically brought her up," the older girl said long afterward. Catherine had been bowled over from the beginning by this marvelous, rash, reckless child, who somehow managed to give a golden glow to the lives of everyone around her. It was not simply that Thérèse's stories offered a romantic future in which they would all end up rich. Her dreams of splendor were not at this stage primarily material-istic. She opened up possibilities that were ampler, freer, and incomparably more exciting than the dull daily grind available in Aussonne. It was a lib-erating vision, and Catherine committed herself to it with the passionate intensity of a nature that needed to serve some purpose larger than her own immediate concerns. Before the two ever left their village, they had laid the foundations of a pact that would carry them triumphantly through twenty years of struggle to heights even Thérèse could hardly have envisaged at the start, before disaster finally engulfed them both.

❧❧❧

Thérèse's tricks and treats added drama, zest, and conspiratorial excitement to her girlfriends' lives. They hatched plots, staged scenes, and mounted charades under her direction. At one point Thérèse persuaded the other girls to pool their bits of jewelry because, as she said with an ingenuous lisp: "People will think I've got bags of jewels, if I change them often enough."

Catherine Fuzié, the bailiff's beautiful daughter,
who believed in Thérèse from the beginning.

Another time, when guests arrived to hear her play the piano, she explained that she was too shy to perform in public, retiring to the next room where a musical friend played the piece for her, whereupon Thérèse modestly reappeared to take her bow. Performances like this one sprang from the sheer love of make-believe and mystification for their own sakes. But they were also practical rehearsals for the far more elaborate conjuring feats Thérèse would pull off in later life. "She was still so young in those days," said an observer, "that people just laughed at her showing off, and her childish lies."

Thérèse was following in the footsteps of her father, who had returned to his old dreams of a noble ancestry and a lost heritage, claiming to have proofs of both in the chest full of yellowing parchment that, according to Thérèse, dominated her childhood. A locked coffer containing crucial documents would be a constant element in the games Thérèse played out ever afterward, along lines laid down early by her father. In her teens and early twenties she talked often about a legacy from a mysterious well-wisher. Sometimes the donor was a retired village schoolmistress, living a day's drive

GRANDEUR ET DÉCADENCE DE MADAME HUMBERT    (1)

Thérèse in her prime, portrayed in the popular press
as a conjurer pulling rabbits out of a hat in front of the
famous Humbert strongbox, said to contain a fortune.

*(Photo: © Collection Viollet, Paris)*

away in Rabastens, or a godmother from Le Havre. Once it was a rich Dutch aunt. Perhaps Thérèse's imaginary bequest had something to do with her mother's failure to inherit Farmer Duluc's money; and perhaps her string of phantom benefactors played variations on her real aunt, her mother's wealthy sister Madame Dupuy, who in fact made no move to help her hard-up nieces and nephews. Madame Dupuy came in handy instead as a figment of Thérèse's consoling fictions. The barber Bérard, whose father had been one of Duluc's many creditors, said that, even as a small girl, Thérèse could always wheedle a loan out of him by promising to get her Aunt Dupuy to honor her grandfather's outstanding debts.

All her life Thérèse treated money as an illusion: a confidence or conjuring trick that had to be mastered. In the years of poverty that followed her mother's death, she never let lack of funds stand in her way. Wild rumors about her father now began to be outdone by wilder ones about his daughter. "I'd always heard talk of the Daurignacs," said Bérard, who followed the family's fortunes avidly, regularly tuning in with the rest of the neighbors

DEFENSE D'OUVRIR !!!

1. — Ils sont là !!!...

Another popular cartoon showing Thérèse with her locked strongbox and one of her dream castles in the background.
*(Photo: © Collection Viollet, Paris)*

to catch the latest episode in a soap opera that seemed altogether too well plotted for real life. Thérèse galvanized the whole countryside with her escapades, excursions, and flirtations. Never exactly pretty, she prided herself when young on a neat waist, slender ankles, and a trim figure. She looked her best in a close-fitting riding habit that mesmerized the young farmers for miles around. She planned picnics and riding parties, gave dinners and musical evenings, borrowed a coach for pleasure trips that nobody ever forgot.

Her reputation spread first to nearby villages like Beauzelle and Blagnac, then to Toulouse itself. People had never known anything like it. Thérèse's wide-eyed innocence was especially disarming. She gave the impression of being constantly surprised by everything. Even the most suspicious were captivated by her trustfulness and evident lack of guile. She had the hesitant, husky, seductive voice of the true *Toulousaine*, and her lisp made her irresistible. "As we say in these parts," wrote another compatriot: "You would have given her the Good Lord without hearing her confession."

Certainly the dressmakers, bootmakers, hatters, and hairdressers of Toulouse were no match for the young Thérèse. "I'll pay you [*Ze vous paierai*]," she said with her ingenuous air and her adorable lisp: "I'll pay you as soon as I get my inheritance." When her debts mounted to such dizzy heights that the tradespeople's resistance stiffened, she staged her most ambitious coup to date: Thérèse was seventeen when she announced her engagement to the son of a Bordeaux shipping magnate, explaining in floods of tears that it was a loveless match she must force herself to go through with in order to honor a pact made in her infancy between their two fathers. She wept so piteously that it was only after an elaborate trousseau had been ordered, made to measure, and delivered to Aussonne, that the Toulouse shop-keepers slowly realized they had been diddled once again. Since there was no fiancé, there would be no wedding, and no well-heeled father-in-law to pick up the tabs.

It was this affair that tipped the scale. Tradesmen, who had put up with being tricked and exploited for years, rose up together in revolt. Streams of creditors, duns, and bailiffs converged on L'Oeillet. Bankruptcy could no longer be staved off. By 1874 the family was in the hands of the receiver, their house sold and its contents repos-sessed. The Daurignacs left Aussonne in disgrace to look for work in Toulouse. The two elder boys found low-grade jobs, Emile as a piano salesman,

The city of Toulouse, where Thérèse practiced and perfected the magical art of true romance.

Romain as a shop assistant. Ten-year-old Louis was packed off to a school run by Trappist monks. Places were arranged for the two little girls at an academy, where their bills were seldom paid at the end of the school term.

Thérèse, powerless to prevent the family's ruin and dispersal, was now publicly dependent on the uncertain charity of creditors. Each morning she stopped off with her empty shopping basket to touch Monsieur Bérard for a few coins with which to see herself and her father through the day. "I couldn't let them starve," he said, "so I always gave her something. Even reduced to penury, she still kept the airs of a young lady." She rented wretched rooms with a few sticks of broken furniture high up under the roof of a cheap lodging house in the rue de Taur. Thérèse's motto in later life was a flat statement: "What I want, I will have [*Je veux, j'aurai*]." To some it smacked of ruthless greed. But to people who had known her in these years of humiliation and defeat—when she had failed to keep a roof over the children's heads and could no longer even be sure where their next meal was coming from—it seemed more like whistling in the dark.

❧✣❧

**None of her** Toulouse relatives wanted anything to do with a family that had brought fresh shame to the already notorious name of Daurignac.

Besides Madame Dupuy, Thérèse had a second aunt, another of Farmer Duluc's penniless bastards, who had started out in the 1850s by earning her living as a maid. Marie-Emilie Thénier (or Tenière) had worked at 3, rue de Pomme, in the same house as her half-sister, Thérèse's mother, Rosa Daurignac, who sold lingerie on the ground floor. Both sisters were forceful, brave, and energetic, but it was the maid of all work who pulled off what turned out to be by far the more advantageous match. Marie-Emilie married the young law teacher whose lodgings she looked after above the shop in the rue de Pomme. Her husband was Gustave Humbert, a highflier with political ambitions who became Professor of Roman Law at the University of Toulouse, going on ten years later to be elected to the House of Representatives in Paris as the local deputy for Haute-Garonne.

The Humberts had two children, Frédéric and Alice, who were roughly the same age as their cousins Thérèse and Emile Daurignac. The four children grew up together. Thérèse by her own account was the childhood sweetheart of her cousin Frédéric, who wooed her with a ring made of polished tin. Even after Deputy Humbert moved to Paris to further his political career, he brought his family back every summer to the country outside Toulouse. They had a house beside the church at Beauzelle, where Frédéric's father quickly singled out the clever young schoolmaster, Armand Parayre, whose wife, Catherine, had been Thérèse's great friend in Aussonne. Parayre became Humbert's confidential secretary and Latin tutor to young Frédéric.

❧❦❧

**The Humberts' fortunes** rose in the early 1870s as the Daurignacs' went downhill. Deputy Humbert was one of the constitutional pioneers who laid the foundation stones for the Third Republic, after France's catastrophic defeat by Germany at the start of the decade. The new republic represented a fresh start for the whole country: a modern, secular, democratic state liberated at last from the stranglehold of the Roman Catholic Church as well as from the imperial folly that had ended with the downfall of Napoleon III.

Thérèse's uncle, Senator Gustave Humbert,
who rose to be the Third Republic's most
celebrated minister of justice.

Deputy Humbert was made a senator, or life member of the newly established upper house, in 1875.

Young Frédéric was seventeen years old that year, studying law in his first term at Toulouse University, where his fellow students remembered him as a dull, bookish lad with artistic leanings. He founded a literary review for which his cousin

Emile Daurignac wrote articles. Frédéric was not stupid, but he was timid: in every way a paler, feebler, flatter version of his father. It was Thérèse who shone. Thérèse had a will to match her uncle's, and the enterprise to make the most of it. All their lives she would be the fixed post for Frédéric's clinging vine. Thérèse was eighteen, and destitute in 1875. She had also lost her power base. For the first time she found herself discredited imaginatively as well as financially in the eyes of everyone she knew. Drastic action was called for.

Four years after the Daurignac disaster, Thérèse and her brother Emile married the two young Humberts in a double wedding at Beauzelle.

The wedding celebrations on September 7, 1878, were by far the grandest spectacle the village had ever seen. People still talked about them well into the next century. The houses were decked with flowers, triumphal arches spanned the street, and the whole countryside turned out to watch the carriage procession. These were the first carriages to reach Beauzelle (which was not much more than a collection of market gardens beside the Garonne River), and the horses had to be unharnessed so that the bridal coach could be hauled by hand up the steep slope to the church. Guns were fired and bonfires lit. Peasants poured in to join the dancing.

The two brides, together with their attendants, were sumptuously attired by a team of seamstresses working under Madame Bérard, the barber's wife, who traveled up to Paris to check out the latest fashions. The top tailors, glovers, milliners, and shoemakers of Toulouse, suppressing painful memories of the earlier Daurignac fiasco, toiled over Thérèse's wedding outfits. The Bérards' bill alone came to nearly five thousand francs (enough to rent a luxury apartment in Paris for a year). None of these accounts was ever paid. But, over the next two decades and more, the local shopkeepers came to congratulate themselves on having launched Thérèse in style with a splendor that matched the scale of her subsequent operations on the national stage. Even after her downfall, her sheer nerve inspired a certain perverse pride. As an old man, the barber recounted with something like awe the story of how, on the day she was to leave for her honeymoon, Thérèse arranged to meet him on the station platform as she and her bridegroom boarded the midnight train for Paris so that the entire reckoning could be settled, instead of which he found himself, to his stupefaction, paying off her cabdriver:

Can you believe that I was to pay for her cab—that she'd been driving about in it since the morning—and that it would cost me a mere twenty francs, which I was to add to my account! The twenty francs are still outstanding, incidentally. So that is how—as if it wasn't enough to have dressed her for the wedding—I ended up paying her cab fare as well!

❧

The Humbert weddings puzzled people at the time and afterward. Contemporaries wondered what on earth could have persuaded an outstanding politician, clearly destined for the highest office, to marry off his two underage children to a couple of rascally young scroungers like the Daurignacs. The answer seemed to be the Château de Marcotte. Thérèse's fantasies, like her father's, drew strength from reality's shortcomings. When the real world fell to pieces around her ears, she took refuge in her dream castles, which never let her down. Marcotte's marble terraces and orange groves made up for the hard beds and meager diet in the dismal attics of the rue de Taur. Thérèse liked to think that the property had been left her by one of the kindly spinster aunts who peopled her imagination. She gave this testator different names at different times to different people. It might have been a Mademoiselle Lagourdère, or a Mademoiselle Latrémollière, or then again a Mademoiselle Baylac with usufruct to Mademoiselle Lucas.

There can be no doubt that on some level Thérèse persuaded herself, and perhaps her husband too, that Marcotte genuinely existed. As a student writing home to his mother, Frédéric described baskets of flowers and parcels of game arriving from his fiancée's estate. "At the time of my marriage," said Thérèse, "I believed so completely in Marcotte that we drew up an official power of attorney appointing Monsieur Parayre to run the property." Armand Parayre (who confirmed that he had indeed been named steward of Marcotte) was an eminently practical idealist with no time for fantasy. Determined to devote his life to the great reforming causes that fired his whole generation in France, he had given up any prospect of a more lucrative career in order to help liberate the illiterate masses through education. In his forties he would become a crusading newspaper editor, campaigning for progress, democracy, and the secularization of the state. No one who met him ever doubted his transparent honesty. Marcotte's authenticity could have found no better guarantee than the fact that a man of such unimpeachable integrity was prepared to vouch for it.

Parayre for his part accepted the purely honorary stewardship of a place neither he nor anyone else ever set eyes on because it was in the gift of Senator Humbert. The post was a sign of favor from a national figure who, for young radicals like Parayre, embodied the loftiest aspirations of the nascent Third Republic.

Humbert had impeccable credentials. His father had taken part in the French Revolution of 1789, and he himself had manned the barricades as a young man defending the republican tradition when street fighting broke out again in 1848. In Toulouse in the 1870s he attracted a band of ardent youths who looked to him for leadership in the ongoing struggle against reaction. They included

Armand Parayre, the idealistic young village
schoolmaster who married Catherine Fuzié,
going on to become a radical newspaper editor
and key figure in the Humbert empire in Paris.
*(Collection Gaetana Matisse)*

Parayre and his brothers, young Frédéric with his
Daurignac cousins, and the son of another university law professor, Arthur Huc, himself a distinguished future journalist in the proud left-wing tradition of the town. All of them were socialists,

free-thinkers, and Freemasons: passionate believers in the republican ideals that came under increasing threat toward the end of the century from the resurgent right wing. Parayre and his contemporaries longed to unite once more beneath the Revolution's proud banner of Liberté, Egalité, Fraternité. They marched, as France's top Freemason put it, "in the vanguard of the armies of progress" with good old Papa Humbert at their head.

But, if the senator was to become a power in the land by taking his rightful place among the new republican elite, he would need to keep up a certain state. Humbert had no money of his own (his father had been a small wine merchant in Metz before the German army seized Alsace-Lorraine from France). Even the noblest and most disinterested political program needs financing, and a daughter-in-law with a substantial dowry offered a possible way of doing it. Thérèse's detractors at the end of her career cast her as a scheming trickster who had invented a fraudulent inheritance expressly in order to trap the unsuspecting Frédéric and his rather more sagacious father. Frédéric's own mother threw her considerable weight behind this view, vigorously denouncing her niece as "the wretch who stole my son" (the two women had a history of mutual dislike, presumably going back to the fact that each knew too much about the other's origins for comfort). By this time Senator Humbert had died, passing into legend as a republican secular saint. Few cared to scrutinize his past too closely or to pick holes in the case for his defense put up by his doughty widow.

But people in Toulouse remembered the senator sounding out potential backers about the prospect of raising money in advance on his daughter-in-law's estate. Within a few years of the marriage, Humbert personally arranged to mortgage Marcotte on the strength of three bonds—testifying apparently to a value of 780,000 francs—which Thérèse fished out of her bodice at his signal in the presence of four witnesses (including the lawyer who later described the scene in court). Marcotte was not the only deal Humbert brokered for Thérèse. He was equally involved with another nonexistent estate, this time a plantation of cork oaks in Portugal, with a history very similar to Marcotte's.

❧❧❧

Louis Daurignac remembered talk of his sister's Portuguese inheritance even before the family left Aussonne. He thought the property came from Thérèse's old schoolmistress in Rabastens. Others believed it had been left her by a Portuguese friend of her mother's: a passerby who had collapsed with a heart attack in the rue de Pomme, breaking Madame Daurignac's glass shopwindow. When she nursed him back to health, he repaid her with a legacy to her little daughter (who was also perhaps his own). In 1874—the year the Daurignacs lost everything—a Senhor R. A. died in Lisbon, according to Thérèse, leaving his estate to her. She said she had heard the news from the Portuguese consul in Toulouse. From then on she kept the title deeds stuffed in her blouse, but her fellow citizens remained unimpressed, and the possibility of obtaining a mortgage in the estate of Sabatou-Blancou never got off the ground. It would be another eight years before the Portuguese property brought in a serious sum.

Senator Humbert had achieved the summit of his ambition in January of that year, when he was appointed keeper of the seals, or minister of justice. He had finally become a prince of the new republican aristocracy. The first business acquaintance to whom he mentioned his daughter-in-law's Portuguese inheritance—a Doctor Fourès of Coursan, near Narbonne, in the southwest of France—leaped at the chance to advance him sixty thousand francs (the rough equivalent of $200,000 today). It would have been absurd at the time to question the good faith of a man who had just been appointed to the highest legal office in the land. But twenty years later, almost a decade after Humbert's death, when a police search failed to locate either Marcotte or Sabatou-Blancou, doubts crept in. Humbert was a shrewd negotiator celebrated throughout France for his grasp of legal strategy and tactics. Even supposing that the brain that wrote the constitution of the Third Republic could initially have been fooled by an unsophisticated girl with no legal background whatsoever, it was hard to credit that the minister could have gone on being her dupe.

Nobody apparently realized, then or later, that the two were uncle and niece. Once they had left Toulouse, both parties studiously concealed their relationship. Neither Thérèse nor any of the Humberts ever admitted that she and her husband were first cousins, or that the minister of justice had known her from the days when he lived in lodgings above her mother's shop. Over the years he had seen Thérèse develop from a child with a talent for artless make-believe into a performer who could virtually hypnotize hardheaded shop-keepers like Bérard. "What gave her her power was her astonishing fertility of invention," the bar-ber himself explained in retrospect,

> and above all her staggering, superlative audacity! She would ask you the most pre-posterous favors in such a natural way that you accepted them as natural too, and never realized you'd been had until it was too late. She played some shocking tricks on me, even when I thought I knew her well.

Thérèse's creative gift was spontaneous and natural. "She lied as a bird sings," said a witness who knew her in her prime. She combined the psychological subtlety of an experienced actor with a novelist's narrative exuberance. If she had chosen books, instead of real life, as the medium for her romantic fictions about missing deeds, locked coffers, surprise legacies, and long-lost parents, she would have been a nineteenth-century bestseller. There was nothing calculating to start with about her absurd, implausible, and hopelessly inconsistent fabrications. It was only gradually that the dream castles described in such loving circumstantial detail were replaced by relatively prosaic but portable, easily concealable (and eminently forgeable) bearer bonds. The plot was skillfully streamlined, and the multiple, hydra-headed, perpetually changing benefactors narrowed down to one. The process took place in the five years following Thérèse's marriage, which were also the five years in which her Uncle Humbert played for the highest stakes of his career.

❧❦❧

The senator was said to have been the first to give the unlikely name of Crawford to his daughter-in-law's Portuguese well-wisher. In Thérèse's own

The CRAWFRAUD INHERITANCE, or The Secrets of a Strongbox:
one of many cartoons depicting the opening of the strongbox said to
contain Thérèse's Crawford legacy. *(Bibliothèque des Arts Décoratifs,
Paris, all rights reserved; photo: © Jean-Loup Charmet, Paris)*

version, Crawford was an English milord who happened to fall ill in the very lodging house where she
was living in Toulouse. Like her mother before her,
she tended this passing stranger on his sickbed in
the rue de Taur, where he eventually died, but not
before drawing up a will in his nurse's favor. This

will was inscribed on a marble slab inlaid in Crawford's bedroom wall: a virtuoso touch that got Thérèse into such trouble with troublesome customers who wanted to walk up and inspect the wall that Milord's death had to be relocated three hundred miles eastward to Nice.

Thérèse told this story to all comers, adding "with a stammer and tears in her eyes that her mother had enjoyed a very close relationship with the man who had just died, making her his heir." It was characteristic of Thérèse's new and worldlier approach that Crawford was now clearly understood to have been her mother's lover, with the implication that she herself was his natural daughter. Signs of her old careless, prodigal inventiveness surfaced in a story she told Catherine Parayre, about how the Daurignacs had once rescued a child from the clutches of a kidnapper at the Pyrenean resort of Bagnères-de-Bigorre (or could it have been Bagnères-de-Luchon?), where the colossally rich and lavish Crawford happened to be staying. In yet another variation Crawford was an American whose life she saved after an accident in what must have been a phenomenally early motor car. Details from these and other experimental drafts fed into the final master text, which featured an American millionaire called Robert Henry Crawford, who died at Nice on September 7, 1877 (a year to the day before the Beauzelle weddings), having signed the usual will the day before, naming Thérèse as sole beneficiary. This last and best of all her benefactors left her a princely one hundred million francs (about a third of a billion dollars today).

"What demonstrates above all else the genius of Thérèse," wrote an old friend (who only ever identified herself as "Madame X"),

> is the grandeur, the sheer immensity of the scale on which she operated. If she had laid claim to an inheritance of no more than four or six million, she would not have lasted two years, and would with difficulty have managed to raise a miserable few thousand francs. But a *hundred million*! People took their hats off to a sum like that as they would have done before the Pyramid of Cheops, and their admiration prevented them from seeing straight.

Cartoon showing the imaginary Crawford family gathered for the reading of the will. *(Bibliothèque des Arts Décoratifs, Paris, all rights reserved; photo: © Jean-Loup Charmet, Paris)*

Scale, simplicity, and orderly arrangement were central to the story that emerged, once Thérèse's rampant fantasies had been edited and authorized by the combined legal intelligence of the Humberts, father and son. The two were said to have spent weeks or even months together in the summer of 1883, holed up in a country retreat outside Paris, refining the details of a scheme that was already well on the way to a radical repackaging of the family's finances.

The change came none too soon for the young Humberts, who had spent their first two years of married life in Paris at 68, rue Monge among the squalid cafés, cheap wineshops, and fly-by-night lodging houses of the Latin Quarter. They survived from hand to mouth on heavy borrowings, heavier debts, and occasional handouts from Frédéric's father. Thérèse was used to dodging duns and bamboozling bailiffs with court orders, but her husband had to learn from scratch. When Thérèse became pregnant, her two younger sisters came up from Toulouse to camp out in the attics of the rue Monge with their aged father. Auguste Daurignac—or d'Aurignac as he now liked to be known—was in his eightieth year in 1880, when his daughter presented him with his first grandchildren, twin babies, one of whom died at birth. The family moved that year with the survivor, a girl called Eve, into better lodgings near the Opéra on the Chaussée d'Antin.

The young Humberts' upward mobility accelerated into top gear with Frédéric's father's nomination, on January 30, 1882, as justice minister in the cabinet formed by Charles Freycinet after the fall of Léon Gambetta. They bought a whole house, or *hôtel particulier*, that January, on the rue Fortuny, behind the fashionable Parc Monceau, where they kept four servants as well as a carriage and horses of their own. Two months later they acquired an even grander country residence near Melun, in the forest of Fontainebleau, fifteen miles south of Paris. The Château de Vives-Eaux was the first of Thérèse's real-life dream castles: a mock-Gothic pile set in a wooded park above a series of pools on the lawns below the house, descending to a private lake linked by a broad channel to the Seine.

❧❧❧

Frédéric was by now installed as his father's principal private secretary, or *chef de cabinet*. Emile Daurignac and Armand Parayre came up to Paris with their families to join the new minister's train. Political dinners at the *hôtel* in the rue Fortuny, and weekend house parties at Vives-Eaux, were organized by Armand's wife, Catherine, and hosted by Frédéric's wife, Thérèse. These were the performances for which they had rehearsed as girls at village hops and country dances in Aussonne. Thérèse adapted effortlessly to the social showmanship and conspicuous consumption of the Parisian Belle Epoque, easily eclipsing her sober middle-aged aunt Humbert and her retiring cousin Alice (who was her sister-in-law twice over), in the role of the minister's unofficial hostess. She set herself to woo the cream of republican high society just as she had once bewitched the farmers of Haute-Garonne. Young Madame Humbert, with her breathy voice, her Toulouse accent, and her charming little lisp, proved a credit to her father-in-law. Even the most supercilious Parisians were

Frédéric Humbert as *chef de cabinet* in the Ministry of
Justice: The sharp legal brain of Thérèse's shy and self-
effacing husband smoothed her path behind the scenes.

*(Photo: © Topham Picturepoint)*

beguiled by the freshness of her frankly rustic manners, and by her air of longing to learn what they had to say. They were still more intrigued by the piquant rumors beginning to circulate about her supposedly fabulous wealth.

If the story of Thérèse's inheritance needed to be tried out in many different drafts before it could be established on a sound business footing as a money-making concern, so did the practical machinery. At the beginning of 1883, the young Humberts traveled south, staying at the best hotel in Narbonne with a retinue of courtiers and attendants. Word got around that rich pickings were to be had. The great heiress with her ministerial connections in Paris was courted by eager lawyers, speculative financiers, land agents, and landowners only too anxious to lend money or, alternatively, sell off their assets. The Crédit Foncier chipped in with nine hundred thousand francs. Other banks and businesses between them advanced as much again.

The Humberts now disposed of capital on a scale previously unimaginable by anyone except perhaps Thérèse. She herself had made a triumphal return to Toulouse the year before, in order to deposit sixty thousand francs with the Banque de France, announcing that it was the revenue from her Portuguese cork oaks. Even her great expectations had grown by leaps and bounds since then. "The inheritance inflated in front of your eyes, it mounted up into the millions," said a witness, describing good old Papa Humbert's method of bidding up advances on a legacy that had started out at no more than a paltry few hundred thousand francs. "It was no longer an inheritance. It was a geometrical progression."

❧❧

The main business of the visit to Narbonne made all previous transactions look small. The Humberts spent months negotiating the purchase of the Château de Celeyran, the ancestral home of the Comtesse de Toulouse-Lautrec (whose son Henri, painting landscapes at Celeyran that summer, would shortly galvanize Montmartre with his eye-catching posters of raunchy cabaret stars). Celeyran changed hands on March 29, 1883, for two million francs, a sum that made people's eyes grow wide. All of it was borrowed. A Monsieur Bagnères lent 1.6 million francs (which the Humberts would repay only after years of lawyers' threats, judicial writs, bailiffs' raids, and a final lawsuit). The estate was to be mortgaged and stripped of its assets, including the fine wines from its vineyards (bottled and sold from now on by the Humberts' wine merchant in Melun). None of the family ever lived there. The property was managed first by Armand Parayre's brother-in-law, Jacques Boutiq, and later by his brother, Alexandre Parayre. Its prime importance was as an advertising investment which boosted the Humberts' credit, bringing in handsome profits from lenders throughout their native region.

The Narbonne spending spree set a pattern that would serve the Humberts well for the next two decades. Spectacular display, speedy exploitation, and colossal turnover were their watchwords. One of many puzzles, for those who tried to analyze the workings of the scheme in retrospect, was its initial funding. Start-up capital—enough to set up the establishment on the rue Fortuny, and make the first confidence-building bank deposits—must have come from somewhere. The answer once again lay with Justice Minister Humbert. His first move on taking office had been to supervise the winding up of the Union Générale Bank, which had collapsed, causing panic on European stock markets in January 1882. Shares had been virtually wiped out by January 30, when Humbert put the bank's affairs in the hands of the public prosecutor, who promptly arrested its founder, Eugène Bontoux. The bank was declared bankrupt three days later, ruining thousands of investors (including the great pioneering art dealer, Paul Durand-Ruel, who had been for many years the impressionists' only backer).

The Union Générale was a speculative venture, set up expressly to undermine the Rothschild Bank (which helped the government resolve the stock market crisis by massive transfers of capital). Funds came from the anti-Semitic, pro-Catholic, royalist right wing, rallying behind what looked like a vigorous new thrust in the campaign to topple the still young and shaky Third Republic. The Union Générale's failure was hailed as a public triumph for Humbert, for the Rothschilds, and for the republican cause in general. But shortly after the crash, the new minister secretly deposited large sums (some said as much as two million francs) in various private accounts. One of them was with the Comptoir d'Alsace, whose director, Léopold Sée, saw this windfall as a payoff from the Rothschilds. Sée and others maintained that Thérèse Humbert had supplied a timely alibi for her father-in-law's otherwise inexplicable access of capital.

Although Humbert lost his ministry with the fall of Freycinet's cabinet in July 1883, the family fortunes continued to rise. The former minister retired to Vives-Eaux, saying he meant to sort out his daughter-in-law's inheritance ("I'm going to have my work cut out clearing up the death duties"). At the beginning of the summer the legacy in question was reported to be 1.5 million francs from Thérèse's Le Havre godmother. By the time Humbert left Vives-Eaux to return to Paris, the testator's identity had changed, and the sum had multiplied more than sixtyfold into the Crawford millions.

That autumn the young Humberts bought a newspaper: *L'Avenir de Seine et Marne,* which Armand Parayre would run for the next decade as a rip-roaring radical organ, laying into all enemies of progress and masterminding Frédéric's election as the republican deputy for Melun. In 1884 two more estates near Melun, Orsonville and Villiers-en-Bière, were added to the Humbert portfolio. The year after that Thérèse gave a housewarming party, marked by what even hardened Parisians saw as unheard-of luxury, to celebrate her family's final move into the most splendid of all the properties she ever owned, at 65, avenue de la Grande Armée.

The avenue de la Grande Armée was a continuation of the Champs-Elysées, running westward from the Arc de Triomphe through the cliffs and ravines of monolithic apartment buildings put up to house the new men—bankers, entrepreneurs, speculative developers—who were the architects of modern Paris. Baron Haussmann's scheme for urban renewal meant tearing down whole districts of the capital to make way for spacious vistas along broad avenues lined with imposing, even futuristic buildings. Paris in the closing decades of the nineteenth century saw an explosion of energy and confidence in some ways comparable to what would happen in the United

The mansion at 65, avenue de la Grande Armée
where Thérèse made her dreams come true.
*(Photo: © Topham Picturepoint)*

States in the 1920s. Industrialists who built rail-roads, mechanized production, and pioneered the first department stores turned the old social, financial, and cultural certainties upside down. Innovation and experiment were at a premium. New money backed new ideas, whether it meant installing gas lighting, astounding passersby with the latest iron-framed glass architecture, or buying the impressionist paintings that scandalized less forward-looking contemporaries. The reforming vision of the Third Republic went hand in hand with capital expansion, rich returns on rash investment, and a thirst for novelty that made Paris fashions the envy of the world.

No one exemplified the twin goals of this new world—democratic progress and prodigal display—more exuberantly than young Madame Humbert. She was not yet out of her twenties when she finally moved with her family into the castle of her dreams in 1885. Her very naïveté was as crucial as her persuasive powers to the smooth working of her father-in-law's scheme. If investors were to gain confidence in this particular illusion, Thérèse must indulge to the full all the cravings suppressed but not stifled by her penurious past.

She embodied not only her own but other people's dreams. Like a 1920s Hollywood movie star, she aimed to make the public gasp at the sumptuous extravagance of her lifestyle.

Thérèse's new house on the avenue de la Grande Armée was known in the Humberts' circle as "the Château." Its massive portals opened onto vestibules, antechambers, and a waiting room furnished with antique guns and musical instruments, where visitors waited to be summoned before climbing the marble staircase to the palatial apartments on the second floor: the billiard room, the dining room, and the great studio, or salon, stuffed with silk upholstery, fine old carvings, Gothic sideboards, bronzes, silverware, and cloisonné enamels. In these gilded halls, hung with priceless tapestries and furnished with Renaissance thrones and chests, Thérèse could at last play out her childhood scenario of a world richer, grander, more clear-cut and more highly charged than anything real life had to offer.

"Anyone who was anyone in politics, at the bar, in the courts, the government, and the world of high finance ended up at the Humberts' house," wrote Madame X, who went there herself most days. Three successive presidents of the republic, and at least five prime ministers, were Madame Humbert's personal friends. The populist hero General Boulanger made her house his second home, in his heyday regularly arriving with a train of hangers-on headed by his majordomo. In the mid-1890s President Casimir-Pierre Périer himself presided over one end of Madame Humbert's dining table with Henri du Buit, the leader of the Paris bar, seated at the other. Archbishops, ambassadors, bankers, cabinet ministers, dukes, and diplomats attended her parties and receptions. Her box at the Opéra was crammed. Her guest lists appeared in the next morning's papers. Lines of carriages filled the broad street before her door.

Her short, upright, already thickening, and stoutly upholstered figure took on a semiregal bearing. She favored high-piled, crownlike hats, surmounted by rearing confections of fruit, birds' nests, or peacock feathers. Madame Humbert's headgear and the costumes that went with it made all Paris stare, not always sympathetically ("she looked like a reliquary, stuck all over with jewels," Madame X wrote tartly). The capital's finest jew-

La Grande Thérèse, with her husband and only daughter,
in one of the hats that made all Paris gasp.
*(Photo: © Jean-Loup Charmet, Paris)*

elers competed to satisfy her passion for precious
stones, sending around on approval the bags of
diamonds, emeralds, and sapphires she had longed
for as a girl. Her dresses came from Jacques
Doucet or the Maison Worth (in a single year she
ran up bills with each of 97,000 and 32,000 francs,
respectively).

❧

Thérèse was staging the performance of her
life, and it was essential to the success of the whole
production that she herself, her house, and everything in it—including the guests—should be of
first-class quality. She knew the top people, and
was dressed by the most sought-after couturiers
and modistes. She patronized the best antiquari-
ans, the most fashionable decorators, and the ritzi-
est picture dealer (Georges Petit, the man who
made a fortune out of the impressionists after
Durand-Ruel lost everything to the Union
Générale Bank).

But Thérèse never felt entirely at ease with
anyone except her extended family—brothers, sis-

ters, Toulouse trusties—who knew that the whole enchanted castle was a game of make-believe. She depended absolutely on the clan (*la tribu*), which had followed her to Paris from her hometown, where all of them had begun by sitting at the feet of good old Papa Humbert. Chief among them was the inconspicuous Frédéric, who gave up politics after a few years to dabble in the arts instead, writing playlets, publishing a slim volume of verse, taking painting lessons from one of the leading Salon practitioners of the day, Ferdinand Roybet. Frédéric's role was to oversee the smooth working of the scheme set up by his father, and he played it in private with admirable efficiency. In public the world wrote him off as a weakling, wholly under his wife's thumb. Certainly he seems never to have looked at another woman, and Thérèse, unexpectedly prudish when it came to marital infidelity, loudly proclaimed her devotion to him. Her imagination shied away from sexual involvement: She got her kicks from a different kind of power.

❧❧❧

Emotional support came from her old confidante, Catherine Parayre. As Thérèse's second-in-command, Madame Parayre ran the household with a staff of twenty under her, and a budget of two hundred thousand francs a year. She made a formidable chatelaine, straight backed, stiff necked, and tight lipped, inspiring terror in all those who tried and failed to gain entrance to 65, avenue de la Grande Armée. Next in order of importance was Romain Daurignac, who dealt with new arrivals (apart from guest celebrities) once they had gotten past the dragon at the door. Romain was the joker of the family. Short, dark, and handsome, black-mustached, a smooth talker with a flair for witty one-liners, he traveled all over France on his sister's business and kept a girl in every town. But he also had a darker side. If Frédéric was the brains of the production, Madame Parayre the house manager, and Thérèse the undoubted star, Romain was in charge backstage, where unseen strings were pulled, levers operated, and traps sprung. He had his own quarters in a wing behind the house, with a separate entrance opening on the rue Pergolèse, next to the coach house, yard, and stables at the back.

His brother Emile—solid, bearded, looking older than his thirty years—lent respectability to the outfit. He lived out, sharing a comparatively modest apartment in the rue de Rivoli with his wife, two small children, and his elderly parents-in-law. Gustave Humbert had been appointed vice president of the Senate after he left the Ministry of Justice, becoming a high court judge in 1889, and Chief Justice of the Cour des Comptes (Audit Office) the year after. Venerable and venerated, loaded with honors by a grateful nation, he gave the family enterprise not only legal expertise, but the priceless asset of his great name and reputation.

The three elder Daurignac siblings had always operated as a unit to which the next two—Louis and Marie-Louise—never quite belonged. As children they were too young, and as adults, too recalcitrant. Louis, who had rejected Thérèse's plan for him to join the Trappists, was generally agreed to be the only honest Daurignac. He would have nothing to do with his sister's stage machinery, and she dealt with him as ruthlessly as she treated anything that bugged her: by banishing him, her, or it, physically or mentally, and going on as if there had never been a problem. In Louis's case she simply bought a colonial property in Tunisia and shipped him out to run it. A similar fate awaited Marie-Louise, who had defied Thérèse from infancy. A marriage was arranged with Frédéric's cousin Lucien Humbert, who was packed off to become French consul in the Caucasus, where he caught cholera and died, leaving his widow with two small children to support.

Maria, the youngest and most docile of the Daurignacs, had always been Thérèse's pet. She had none of her eldest sister's fire or bite, and she was no great beauty either. But she was slim, willowy, and gentle, with the added attraction of being some sort of heiress in her own right. Thérèse had seen to it from their beginnings in Aussonne (when Maria was said to have come in for a tidy sum under the *curé*'s will) that the occasional minor legacy had her little sister's name on it. Maria had a gift for shy and graceful improvisation, which Thérèse encouraged. Her own daughter, Eve, was still too small, and temperamentally too close to her father, to show much promise in this line. Maria's pliancy made her readily accept direction, but she was enough of a Daurignac to enjoy embroidering her part once she had learned the lines. She became the adoptive daughter of the house, a Humbert princess to be wooed and won by what a contemporary observer called "the

Thérèse's sister, Maria Daurignac, a princess of the house of Humbert wooed by the young and thrusting dauphins of the Third Republic.
*(Photo: © Hulton Getty, London)*

dauphins of the Third Republic." Over the years it sometimes seemed that half the young hopefuls at the Paris bar were suitors for Maria's hand.

❧❧❧

**Old Father Daurignac,** who had been well into his sixties when his youngest child was born, lived just long enough to see the fulfillment of his own and his firstborn's wildest dreams. When the Comte d'Aurignac—for he had finally ennobled himself—died in 1886, the pomp and splendor of his end equaled the wretchedness of his birth eighty-five years earlier. He lay in state in his daughter's house, and was borne round the corner for a solemn funeral at the gleaming, gold-encrusted society church of St.-Honoré d'Eylau. A fantasist to the last, he had made such a drama out of the provisions in his will that, on the night he died, Armand Parayre had to be summoned to mount guard with his revolver over the family safe.

❧❧❧

This legendary strongbox, shrouded in mystery like all the Daurignacs' ancestral coffers, held the secret at the heart of the great house on the avenue de la Grande Armée. In it lay Crawford's fabled hundred million francs in bearer bonds. It occupied its own locked chamber on the third floor, which no one but Monsieur or Madame Humbert ever entered (except for Madame Parayre, who cleaned and polished the strongbox once a week). Every so often a favored visitor—generally an inquisitive or exacting lawyer—might be permitted to peep around the door. More rarely, the safe would be opened just long enough for a major creditor to gaze in respectful silence at the bulky packets filled with the sealed envelopes that contained the hidden treasure. On more than one occasion the family's most faithful agent—Maître Dumort, a prominent provincial solicitor from Rouen—was smuggled into the next room so that he could watch through a crack as Frédéric Humbert and Romain Daurignac undid the wrappings to clip the annual coupons off the bearer bonds.

Each summer, when the family left for vacation at Vives-Eaux, the packets would be transferred to a valise that was brought downstairs before the assembled household and ritually padlocked for the journey to Armand Parayre's wrist. Parayre's loyalty to the justice minister never faltered. Having once identified the new dawn of republican idealism with the Humberts' cause, he served both with the unconditional devotion of a proud and generous nature. Small, wiry, dark haired, and olive skinned, he was apt to catch fire in a blaze of enthusiasm or indignation. He was a pugilist as well as a crack shot, quick on the draw, and skilled in the arts of self-defense. In 1885 he fought and won a duel over press freedom with a rival journalist in Melun. Whenever the honor of the Humberts was at stake, Parayre was the man they sent for to retrieve it.

❧⁂☙

But beneath all the charades, the castle rituals, and ceremonies lay an uglier reality. The Humberts' state apartments gave way at the back to a warren of little rooms, offices, and cells presided over by

Romain. He had been brought up, like his siblings, on Thérèse's stories, but the aspect that appealed to him was not so much their sumptuosity and spectacle as their seamy underside. Romain had a taste for thuggery. He flourished in an atmosphere heavy with menace, secrecy, and violence. He had his lair on the far side of a door concealed in the wall of the great staircase. Lawyers met in these back parts. Angry lenders were fobbed off, tradesmen milked and bilked. "This was the field on which every sort of battle was fought out with infuriated creditors and vengeful suppliers," wrote F. I. Mouthon, the investigative journalist who came in the end to understand the Humberts better than any other contemporary observer. "Romain did not always emerge unscathed from these rough confrontations with marauding passions."

Once he was discovered bleeding on the floor after a fight with Armand's brother, Alexandre, the steward of Celeyran, whose wages had not been paid. Another time the frantic wife of a ruined newspaper proprietor from Melun drew a revolver on Thérèse, whose life was saved only by Romain's deflecting the gunshots through the

The ladykiller Romain Daurignac: Thérèse's
brother, whose taste for thuggery and violence
underpinned the Humbert empire.
*(Photo: © Hulton Getty, London)*

window. The first of these incidents was hushed up ("Romain wound himself in bandages, put up with the pain, and held his tongue"). But the police were called to arrest the unfortunate lady, who spent the better part of the next two years shut up in a Swiss lunatic asylum. The celebrated head of the Paris police force, Louis Lépine, was a devoted friend of Madame Humbert, and the superintendent at the local station—a certain Commissaire Wagram—could be relied on to support the family in affairs like this one.

The number of dissatisfied, often dangerous, sometimes almost unhinged customers demanding their money back increased each year as the workings of the Humberts' scheme screwed down more and more tightly on its victims. Whatever its cost in human misery and despair, the machinery was, technically and legally, elegant in the extreme. Inside the strongbox with its cargo of forged bearer bonds lay four key documents. The first was Robert Henry Crawford's will, dated September 6, 1877, which named Thérèse as sole beneficiary. Next came a second will, signed on the same day, this time leaving everything to be divided equally between Maria Daurignac and the dying millionaire's two American nephews, Robert and Henry Crawford. The third document, dated March 1883, was an agreement by the Crawford brothers to hand over their uncle's entire fortune into Madame Humbert's keeping, on condition that it remain intact until the dispute had finally been settled (the Humberts were to live meanwhile on the annual interest from the bonds). Last was a deed, drawn up eighteen months later, under which the Crawfords consented to waive their claim altogether in return for six million francs in cash, together with Maria's hand in marriage for one or the other brother.

These four documents provided the hinge on which the whole scam turned. The claims of the Crawford nephews, which prevented Madame Humbert from ever actually laying hands on her rightful wealth, admirably explained her unending need for credit. When the Crawfords finally named their price for withdrawing from the field, lenders fell over themselves to supply the triumphant heiress with six million francs at advantageous rates of interest. Madame Humbert's story was that the dastardly Crawfords had refused to take her money, dishonoring their pledge on the pretext that Maria declined to become engaged to either of them. In October 1885 a case against the two brothers was brought before the Civil Tribunal of the Seine, which delivered its verdict a year later in Madame Humbert's favor.

❧

The Tribunal of the Seine was, of course, a real court just as the leading advocates hired to represent each side in this dispute were real lawyers. The Crawfords themselves did not exist, but no court was ever asked to pronounce on the validity of the two wills, or for that matter on the existence of the millions. The point at issue was whether or not the imaginary plaintiffs (neither of whom ever appeared in court) had reneged on their no less imaginary agreement of 1883. Once the court ruled that they had, the way lay open for proceedings that in theory never needed to end. The beauty of it was that *Humbert* v. *Crawford* litigation could—and did—drag on indefinitely, from appeal to counterappeal, tended by the grandest lawyers in the land, as the case rose slowly up through virtually every court in France.

Over the years the Crawfords were promoted from purely imaginary figments to phantoms haunting the Humberts' château, flitting from room to room, glimpsed around a door or through a peephole. From time to time they materialized unexpectedly elsewhere, in or outside Paris. In 1885 they were spotted by a bailiff who served papers on them in the Hôtel du Louvre. Later the same year one of them turned up to brief a barrister in Le Havre. An eyewitness reported an odd scene in which Gustave Humbert urged a tearful Maria Daurignac to give up her love for a flighty foreigner like Robert Crawford. Excitement regularly rose and fell, depending on whether the engagement was reported to be on or off. One evening, just as fifty people were sitting down to table at 65, avenue de la Grande Armée, an enormous Chinese vase was delivered with a fond message for Maria from her American suitor.

Suspense reached a peak with a dinner party billed beforehand as the occasion on which Maria

Humbert mania swept the Paris press when the scandal
eventually broke in 1902: Here Thérèse, with her elegant
younger sister Maria, is greeted by the trial judge disguised
as a cabaret host: "Well, Madame Humbert, have you any
news of the good Monsieur Crawfraud?" *(Bibliothèque des
Arts Décoratifs, Paris, all rights reserved; photo: © Jean-Loup
Charmet, Paris)*

would at last accept a marriage proposal from one or other of the young Crawfords. Maximum publicity surrounded this event, which promised to remove the final obstacle standing between Madame Humbert and her fortune. All Paris was agog. Invitations were fiercely coveted. On the night itself, twenty-five distinguished guests took their seats to watch the supposed Robert Crawford solemnly place a packet of jewels, including a gold ring, at Maria's place. She pushed his offering aside as if she had not seen it. At the end of the first course, he retrieved the ring and tried to place it on her finger. Maria flushed scarlet, thrust his arm away, and rose to her feet, holding all eyes riveted, before bursting into tears and running from the room. "The marriage will have to be postponed again," Madame Humbert announced glumly to her guests.

It was generally agreed in retrospect that Romain and Emile Daurignac must have impersonated the Crawford brothers, who spoke French with what their listeners assumed was an American accent. Neither ever said a memorable word, but the scenes in which they took part were so carefully stage-managed that no more was needed than a bare appearance. Conviction came from the authentic splendor of the setting, the genuine eminence of the guests, above all the presence of the former minister of justice. "His name, his titles and functions meant that he had the police, the courts, and the judicial tribunals in his pocket," wrote a contemporary, "and after his death, the republican prestige of so grand an ancestor went on providing his family with cover for many years." Humbert died at the age of seventy-two in 1894. His bust stood in the Hall of Honor of the Law Faculty at Toulouse University. His state portrait—painted by his son Frédéric, who won a medal for it at the Paris Salon—continued to preside in ermine over the château on the avenue de la Grande Armée.

It was years since Thérèse had taken over from him as director of her own affairs, but his restraining influence had supplied a sobering contact with reality. His death precipitated a series of showdowns, beginning with the liquidation of the Girard Bank, which had been one of the Humberts' major creditors. In February 1895 the bank's president, Paul Girard, called on Madame Humbert in a last desperate bid to persuade her to repay him. She refused, whereupon he pulled a gun and shot at her. When the bullet missed, Girard drove straight back to his office to shoot himself.

His name may not have been the first but it was certainly the most impressive on what Madame Humbert called her suicide register. A receiver called Duret was appointed to look into the affairs of the Girard Bank. The Humberts opened negotiations by trying to bribe him over a friendly dinner that ended in a fistfight with Romain, who called the police. Relations were temporarily patched up, but Duret never forgot or forgave this incident. In May the Humberts were publicly denounced for the first time as crooks by the right-wing scandal sheet, *Libre Parole*. Romain's response was to call in the spy ring he had built up for silencing dissatisfied creditors. "'We've got the man behind the press campaign," he told Duret, "and that will be the end of it, you'll see."

The Humberts' own paper, the republican *L'Avenir de Seine et Marne*, had been wound up with the minister's death the year before, leaving Armand Parayre out of a job. He had served his master faithfully for nearly two decades in return for minimal expenses, drawing no salary and committing his own and his wife's savings to the Humberts' cause. His two young daughters both went out to work at this point. The elder, Amélie, was taken on by her Aunt Nine, her mother's sister, Madame Boutiq, who ran a hat shop on one of the grand boulevards in Paris. The younger, Berthe, became a teacher, like her father, in a village school just outside Toulouse. Still unemployed— and possibly unemployable at fifty-one—their father called at the Humberts' house, to ask for the meager compensation on which they had agreed, only to be shown the door with characteristic brutality by Romain. A scuffle and an exchange of death threats developed into a full-scale duel. The pair fought by English boxing rules at the insistence of Parayre, who left his tormentor with a bloody nose in spite of being the older of the two by fourteen years. The police, summoned as usual by Romain, proved less than cooperative, and no charge was made.

Reinstated in the Humberts' favor, Parayre sailed for Madagascar, where he hoped to bring education to the local people. The island had been overrun the year before by French colonial troops, and Parayre's outspoken criticism of army brutality led to his hasty recall. From the Humberts' point of view, he had at least been safely out of the country during the critical phase of legal proceedings brought against them by Duret on behalf of the Girard Bank. Things looked black for the Humberts during this affair, which took place at Elbeuf, in Normandy, in 1896, with an appeal hearing two years later. Duret had retained the barrister René Waldeck-Rousseau, Léon Gambetta's former associate, himself soon to become president of the republic. Rousseau described the Humbert inheritance in court as "the greatest swindle of the century," a phrase that would come back to haunt the perpetrators ever afterward. Their counsel was Thérèse's old friend Maître du Buit, a legal eagle universally respected "for the austerity of his morals, the sincerity of his republican convictions, his sternness as a barrister, the skill and eloquence of his pleas in court." Maître du Buit opened for the Humberts with the ringing declaration: "I stand before the tribunal armed with nothing but the naked Truth."

His clients survived this dual ordeal by the skin of their teeth with a settlement of two million francs to pay. Money had to be raised urgently on an unprecedented scale. Until now Humbert funds had come mainly from their native South. From the mid-1890s onward, the wealthy industrialists of the North were systematically targeted by lawyers operating out of Rouen and Lille. Many of these lawyers, highly respected in their own communities, entrusted their own personal fortunes to the Humberts' bottomless coffers. Maître Dumort of Rouen gave everything he had, a sum amounting in the end to well over 6 million francs (more like $19 million today). Maître Langlois, who drummed up 1.2 million francs from the Marquis de Cazeaux alone, claimed to have raised 12 million in all.

❧❧❧

**Madame Humbert's** reputation for offering the highest rates of interest in France was increasingly backed up by the undercover activities of her brother's hit men. Romain's propensity for extortion, blackmail, and physical force seems to have had free play after the minister's death. One of Dumort's clients—a major firm of distillers, Schotmann et fils of Lille—advanced 2 million francs in 1896. Three years later the murdered body of Paul Schotmann was discovered on a train from Douai to Lille. Rumor said that he had refused a further loan of 7 million francs (a sum duly handed over after his death by his brother, Jean, and his cousin, Emile Schotmann). Romain was never called to account for this murder, or for the subsequent death of a young nephew, his sister Marie-Louise's son Paul Humbert, who was found hanged after a mysterious raid on his parents' house. The family passed this death off as suicide, but many felt that Romain's violent instincts were once again running out of control.

If so, they were eventually reined in by Madame Humbert, whose taste ran to romantic or comic-opera scenarios rather than to her brother's deadly Grand Guignol. Even at the height of danger, with everything to play for, Thérèse relied on effrontery so bold that few had the nerve to call her bluff. One was the bailiff Quelquejay, cele-

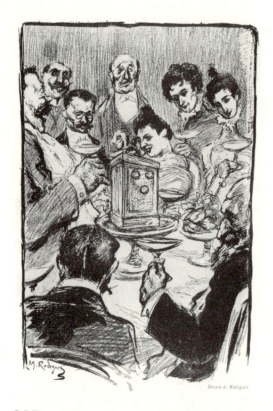

C.I.D. agents toast the Crawfords at a police dinner
given by the Humberts with a chocolate replica of the
famous strongbox in the center of the table.
*(Bibliothèque des Arts Décoratifs, Paris, all rights reserved;
photo: © Jean-Loup Charmet, Paris)*

brated in legend ever afterward as the champion who came nearest to forcibly breaking open the strongbox. People talked in whispers of the day when Madame Humbert personally fought Quelquejay, disputing his papers check by check as she retreated step by step up the great staircase of 65, avenue de la Grande Armée, until sufficient funds arrived in the nick of time to pay him off. Another successful challenger was a minor moneylender who turned up at eight o'clock one morning, seeking repayment of the relatively trifling sum of 250,000 francs, and was put to wait with many others in the music room on the ground floor. "At midday he was still waiting," wrote Mouthon, describing the scene with relish:

> at one o'clock he demolished the piano; at two, he set about the harp and the military trophies; and, in spite of the intervention of Madame Parayre who brought him ten thousand francs from time to time, to calm his nerves and stave off his hunger pangs, he finally stuck his head out of the window with cries of "Stop thief!" and "Fire!" By five o'clock a crowd of a thousand people and

two fire engines had assembled in front of the house. The troublemaker, satisfied with a solid payment on account of one hundred thousand francs, and in any case too smart to risk an encounter with the police, calmly made his escape by the rue Pergolèse, leaving Madame Parayre on the front doorstep, still haranguing the crowd and the firemen.

For once Madame Humbert had met a humorist capable of capping her jokes in her own style. But most of her stooges had to make do with payment in what a contemporary observer called "the small change of hope." Any other sort of change came from Madame Parayre's regular trips to the pawnshop to cash in the week's offerings, mainly from jewelers vying with one another for Madame Humbert's trade. Once she commissioned an elaborate pearl-and-diamond necklace, to be made up at short notice for a friend, including as a mark of special favor jewels from the imperial crown. These were hard to come by (demand had outstripped supply in fashionable circles from the moment the state put them on sale), but the worried jeweler found his problem

Thérèse in her prime: "Ah, what a woman! No one
dared say anything to her, no one dared contradict her,
above all no one dared claim anything back from her!"
(*Photo © Jean-Loup Charmet, Paris*)

solved by a veiled lady who turned up in his shop next day, offering crown jewels for an exorbitant price in cash. The unknown lady was never seen again, and Madame Humbert's necklace was never paid for either. "Ah, what a woman!" said a Humbert employee, "no one dared say anything to her, no one dared caution her, above all no one dared claim anything back from her!"

La Grande Thérèse had emerged from the sticky patch that followed her father-in-law's death with her show firmly back on the road. After the dismissal of the first Girard appeal in 1898, and the silencing of fresh onslaughts in the right-wing press, she looked set for a long run. Critics who had grumbled openly at the beginning now fell silent. "What the Humberts wanted was to give themselves a theatrical décor," wrote Arthur Huc, the Toulouse journalist who had watched the production being tried out in its early stages: "The Humberts recruited more extras than accomplices."

❧❦❧

In the closing years of the nineteenth century, the Humbert show entered its magnificent last act. Art-world celebrities from Sarah Bernhardt to Emile Zola attended Thérèse's parties. The new president, Félix Faure, often dined at 65, avenue de la Grande Armée. The friends and families of his immediate predecessors—Périer and Sadi Carnot— still regularly visited Vives-Eaux for hunting parties in the forest or pleasure trips on the Seine in the Humberts' yacht. Supporters in the police force and the judiciary ranged from Maître du Buit and Police Chief Lépine to the Chief Justice of the Court of Appeals, Frédéric Périer. Madame Humbert could count on solidarity from the republican establish- ment, especially the upper echelons of Freemasonry, traditionally associated with the progressive Left in France.

One of her long-term backers was the attor- ney general, Maître Bulot, who had personally ini- tiated the Daurignacs, Frédéric Humbert, and Armand Parayre as Freemasons in Toulouse almost a quarter of a century earlier. Radical Masons, roped in to support the cause by Parayre, included the hugely popular defense minister, Camille

Pelletan, and the rising young socialist star, Marcel Sembat. Madame Humbert's right-hand man—the nearest she ever came to an official lover or escort—was another Mason, Etienne Jacquin, secretary of the Légion d'Honneur, and chancellor of state at the Ministry of Justice. She traded favors at all levels, from the ministry to the humblest provincial town hall or courthouse. She could arrange for a disgraced magistrate or civil servant to be reinstated; for a prefect to be dismissed; for one creditor's son to be excused from military service, and another's to be pardoned for desertion. "Don't do that," a senior magistrate once said pleasantly to a witness who had threatened to denounce the Humberts. "Don't do that, or I shall be obliged to put you behind bars."

Madame Humbert's position—socially, politically, and from a business point of view—seemed impregnable. The unbeatable rates of interest she offered inspired confidence not only in major finance houses but in thousands of small investors, who had been persuaded to put their money into a new savings bank operating from Romain's back premises on the rue Pergolèse. The Rente Viagère

The Humberts at home. *From left*: Eve Humbert (daughter), Maître du Buit (advocate), Frédéric Humbert (*standing*), Maria Daurignac (*sitting*), Senator Barriere (*standing*), Madame Humbert (*sitting*).
(*Photo: © Mary Evans Picture Library, London*)

had been launched in 1893 on a wholly fraudulent base, with nonexistent capital and a glossy advertising brochure headed by pictures of the pope and President Paul Kruger of South Africa. Business prospered from the start. After three years the enterprise was handed over to Armand Parayre, who ran it as a genuine savings bank with such unexpected flair that, given another ten or twenty years, the Humberts would have been well on the way to becoming authentic millionaires.

**P**arayre celebrated his new job with a wedding party for his elder daughter, Amélie, who was married in January 1898 from 65, avenue de la Grande Armée. Her wedding dress came from Madame Humbert's own couturier, Maison Worth, and Monsieur Humbert signed the register as her witness together with his old colleague from the Ministry of Justice, Councillor of State Jacquin. Her dowry was a bag of jewels, a favorite Humbert wedding present for the children of old friends and supporters. Amélie used hers to buy a year's freedom for herself and her new husband, who was a penniless young painter called Henri Matisse. History does not relate what the Humberts made, if anything, of the strange, brightly colored, increasingly shocking modernistic paintings produced over the next decade and more by the man who married their housekeeper's daughter.

Frédéric Humbert for his part filled the picture gallery on the avenue de la Grande Armée with a very different type of picture, mostly gilt-edged Salon favorites with a sprinkling of old masters. He acquired paintings for the same reason that his wife collected precious stones. "The décor that surrounded the Humberts was designed to produce an illusion for potential clients as well as dazzling their guests," wrote the essayist Jules Claretie:

> The possession of a picture gallery in Paris . . . is an excellent way of establishing your credit. . . . Your standing goes up—like a quotation on the stock exchange—as soon as you put in a bid for a particular canvas. . . . Buying pictures can also be a sound moral investment.

As an index of creditworthiness, Frédéric Humbert's taste could hardly have been more reassuring: Raphael, Delacroix, Corot, and Courbet headed a solid phalanx of now-forgotten society painters—Isabey, Gervex, Baron Gérard—whose prices set new records in their day.

Many of them specialized in history painting, generally felt by nineteenth-century connoisseurs to be the highest form yet achieved by Western art. Humbert was no slouch at it himself, taking a gold medal in 1900 with his *Louis XIII and Mademoiselle de Hautefort* (which was snapped up by the duke of Marlborough, Winston Churchill's cousin, for Blenheim Palace in England). His studio cupboards were stocked with swords, shields, suits of armor, and elaborate medieval costumes for the models. He had set himself up with a luxury bachelor apartment in a studio building on the Place Vintimille, in one of the more sought-after artistic quarters of Paris, where he passed as a painter called Henri Lelong. This was by no means his only false identity. As a student he had signed his articles "Frédéric Haston," and in 1901 he published a slim volume of verse under the name "François Haussy."

Frédéric Humbert as a would-be Salon artist in
the luxuriously equipped studio where he turned out
fashionable history paintings.
*(Photo: © Jean-Loup Charmet, Paris)*

Dressing up, playacting, and impersonation had been a way of life in the Humbert household for so long that even the inmates must sometimes have found it hard to tell what was make-believe and what wasn't. Conspirators regularly disappeared through the concealed door on the grand staircase into Romain's secret lair. Raised voices, slammed doors, and the sound of fistfights or revolver shots gave everyday life an atmosphere more like that of adventure fiction. On one level the real Daurignac brothers played the nonexistent Crawfords. On another Thérèse coached her sister Maria in artificial scenes staged for the benefit of creditors. On a third Frédéric put on a play of his own about a medieval knight who falls in love with a beautiful princess on his way back from the Crusades. The piece was directed by a hired professional and performed in the picture gallery before a fashionable audience. The hero was played by the Humberts' only daughter, Eve, showing off her slender figure in a Crusader's shining armor, with her dashing Uncle Romain cast as a troubadour from Toulouse.

❧❧❧

The turn of the century saw a crescendo of theatrical activity as well as unparalleled ostentation in a household where even the lavatory brushes wore pink satin bows (the bows were purple in Frédéric's studio apartment). But all was not well behind the facade. The strain of keeping up appearances was beginning to tell on the Humberts. "They survived from one day to the next," wrote Arthur Huc, "always in search of fresh credit to clear yesterday's loan, struggling to raise money for the usurer as much as for themselves, reaping little or no benefit from their villainy." Even Thérèse's ingenuity came close to being overstretched. Cornered one day by an importunate dun who turned up with a posse of supporters, she turned at bay, crying, "Take that!" and ripping the necklace from her throat with such force that the string broke, scattering pearls across the floor. The whole household fell to its knees, scrabbling about under the furniture with the bailiffs' men, until the clock struck five when Madame Humbert coolly pointed out that the bailiffs' writ had expired, their time was up, and they must leave, returning any stray pearls as they went.

But by the summer of 1901, odd rumors were starting to fly around Paris. A secret meeting of the Humberts' northern creditors broke up in disarray that autumn. Elie Cattaui of the Anglo-Egyptian Bank sued for repayment of a loan on which he had charged Madame Humbert 64.14 percent interest. In return she accused him of usury. Awkward questions were asked in the national newspapers. *Le Matin* chose this moment to mount a critical campaign, masterminded by F. I. Mouthon with help from the Girard receiver Duret, whose case reached the final Courts of Appeals in Paris early in 1902. People remembered Waldeck-Rousseau's phrase about the greatest swindle of the century. Creditors began to panic. Jacquin and the Humbert lawyers redoubled their denunciation of press calumny and lies. "You can tell how desperate they are by their very fury," Jacquin declared, confidently predicting total vindication for the Humberts. "Many of those who are now howling for their blood will no doubt then be the first to lick their feet."

The end came with a simple request from the appellate judge for the permanent domicile of the elusive Crawford brothers. Madame Humbert gave the first address that came into her head, 1302 Broadway. Investigations in New York reported no Crawfords at any such address. In response to the request of a creditor called Morel, the judge signed an order on Tuesday, May 6, for the strongbox to be opened three days later so that an inventory could be taken of its contents.

That night the Humberts drank a champagne toast, proposed by Thérèse herself with tears in her eyes, to the downfall of their adversaries. The name of Crawford was never mentioned in the Humbert household ("We only ever talked of "Madame's enemies," said Parayre). Thérèse's vivid sense of injury and persecution went back to her own and her family's misfortunes in Aussonne. Tears, help-lessness, a poignant projection of herself as victim were always her trump cards. "I am pursued by vil-lains [*Ze suis poursuivi par les mécants*]," had been her habitual refrain as a wide-eyed girl in Toulouse, trying out the lisp that nobody could resist. "Perhaps she's still saying it," one of her old dupes

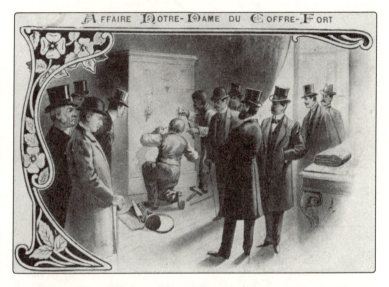

The opening of the strongbox. *(Photo: © Collection Viollet, Paris)*

said drily when Madame Humbert's dreamworld finally collapsed, "with the same faulty pronunciation, and the same air of candor that used to work so well for her."

Thérèse left Paris on Wednesday, May 7, saying she needed a day's rest in the country. Her last act was to send around to her sister-in-law, Alice Daurignac, a watch engraved with her old defiant device—*Je veux, j'aurai*—and a card marked "Pardon!" From that moment she disappeared with her entire family into thin air. Cattaui formally charged her with fraud the next day.

❧❦❧

On Friday, the day set for the opening of the strongbox, crowds began assembling early outside 65, avenue de la Grande Armée. By midday there were ten thousand people in the street, controlled by a police squad under Lépine himself. The man in charge inside the house was the state prosecutor (also a family friend). The Parayres, bewildered by the absence of the Humberts, believed to the last that the safe was about to give up its millions. Locksmiths arrived with hammers when no key could be produced. Du Buit, who had been the last person to say good-bye to Madame Humbert, was among the first to fall back, white-faced and stony-eyed, from the empty strongbox, which contained nothing but an old newspaper, an Italian coin, and a trouser button.

The press grasped instantly that this was the sensational opening episode of a serial or soap

The removal of the strongbox.
*(Photo: © Hulton Getty, London)*

opera likely to run for months. "The *Figaro* can boast of having been present at the most staggering theatrical transformation scene that could have been thought up, even in a Paris so full of strange surprises, preposterous happenings, and absurd buffoonery," wrote the paper's star reporter on May 10, promising to keep his readers up-to-date with each fresh development in "the whole phantasmagoria of this incomparable novel."

Du Buit resigned a week later as leader of the bar, refusing to see or speak to reporters. "What humiliation the man must have endured," wrote Madame X, "having passed for so long as an *eagle* to find that many of his rivals now took him for a *goose.*" Jacquin also tendered his resignation in a humiliating letter (promptly published in the press) to the Minister of Justice, himself another Humbert regular, Monsieur Vallé. The leading lawyers involved on either side in the *Humbert* v. *Crawford* litigation were arrested on suspicion of fraud.

Interviews with shocked, disorientated, sometimes weeping creditors filled the front pages. The Rente Viagère was declared bankrupt. Thousands lost their life's savings. The press published lists, regularly updated, of those to whom the Humberts owed money, together with the staggering sums involved. Names ranged from the Empress Eugénie and the president's son, Paul Loubet, through bankers, lawyers, industrialists, and speculators to the great Parisian jewelers and diamond merchants, Roulina, Haas and Dumaret of the rue de la Paix. The body of a ruined investor called Aloyse Muller, who had committed suicide, was discovered on May 30. Dumaret, to whom Madame Humbert owed nearly two million francs, closed his shop and shot himself two weeks later.

"Scum!" "Cheats and hypocrites!" murmured the fashionable Parisians who piled into Georges Petit's smart art gallery to see the Humberts' picture collection sold that spring. The salesroom was dominated by Frédéric's state portrait of his father, Gustave Humbert (whose bust had already been discreetly removed from the university hall of honor in Toulouse). "All these luxurious leavings stink of grief and ruin, other people's ruin," wrote Jules Claretie, describing the poisonous atmosphere of rancor mixed with gloating among the crowd at Petit's. "You might think that these col-

THÉÂTRE DU PALAIS

LA TROUPE DES
HUMBERT
& Cⁱᵉ 1903

— Venez voir !!! la Femme Colosse THÉRÈSE, le Toupet le plus fort du Monde accompagnée du Nain FRÉDÉRIC, l'eintre, Poète, Musicien, etc., etc., de son frère ÉMILE et du Beau ROMAIN, dans ses poses plastiques.......

"Roll up, roll up!! to see the Female Colossus THERESE, the world's greatest trickster: accompanied by the dwarf FREDERIC, painter, poet, musician, etc., etc., by her brother EMILE and by the handsome ROMAIN, striking a Roman pose. . . . " *(Private collection, all rights reserved; photo: © MT-Giraudon, Paris)* ors had been ground up on the bodies of the victims. And you might ask nervously whether the vermilion in these paintings was mixed with blood."

The Humbert affair loomed over the next weeks and months, raising ominous echoes of the still recent Dreyfus affair. If the first had spelled disaster for the army, the second already looked likely to bring down the judiciary. "The entire public administration of Paris turned pale at the sight of the Humbert dossier," Arthur Huc wrote grimly. An anonymous judge observed that "Madame Humbert would prove a defendant quite as dangerous to others as to herself." People were beginning to wonder why Prefect Lépine (who had successfully organized Dreyfus's arrest) was failing so signally to find any trace of the Humberts. "What power restrains the hand of justice?" asked the *Télégramme* of Toulouse on May 24. "Whose orders have paralyzed the police force?"

The affair was rapidly developing along party lines. The current prime minister, René Waldeck-Rousseau, had been widely regarded by the left as the savior of the republic when he pardoned Captain Dreyfus in 1899. The year before that, Waldeck-Rousseau had been the first to denounce the Humberts in public as swindlers. But by 1902 he was a sick man, worn down by political struggle, with no stomach for taking on a scandal that would tear his party apart and probably destroy the reputation of one of its founding fathers into the bargain. On June 7, exactly a month after the opening of the strongbox, Rousseau was replaced by Emile Combes. A progressive Freemason (at least ten members of Combes's cabinet were Masons), whose chief priority was damage limitation, Combes let it be known that any officious pursuit or agitation would be discreetly discouraged.

❧❀❧

**Madame Humbert** had gone to ground with her husband; her daughter, Eve; and her siblings Emile, Romain, and Maria Daurignac. Sightings of various members of the family, popping up that summer here and there all over Europe, led to nothing. After six months there had been no

The Spanish police eventually discover the Humberts'
hideout. *(Photo: © Mary Evans Picture Library, London)*

progress whatsoever in tracking down the fugitives. On December 6 the matter was raised in the
Chamber of Deputies. Questions were asked as to
why the head of the police force, the attorney
general, and the justice minister—all Humbert
associates—were still holding their jobs. "This was

the signal for the kind of violent uproar we saw
not long ago when questions were asked about the
Dreyfus affair," reported *Le Matin* next day. Fights
broke out among the deputies, developing into
such a riot that the session had to be suspended
three times and finally abandoned altogether.
Right-wingers, who interpreted the Humbert
affair as a left-wing conspiracy, did their best to
implicate Madame Humbert in the Dreyfus scandal, or better still hold her personally responsible
for it, on the grounds that her creditors included
Dreyfus's father-in-law, the diamond merchant
Alfred Hadamard. The charges were taken up
with enthusiasm by the right-wing press ("The
*Sun* made a mistake in not offering a live rabbit
and six dozen macaroons to the joker who can
make any sense of this ludicrous rigmarole," Huc
wrote crisply).

Within two weeks of the parliamentary
brawl, the Humberts were discovered in hiding in
Madrid. Their arrests on December 20 were
reported under banner headlines in the newspapers. Vast crowds assembled at the station on
December 29 to see the family brought back to

Thérèse Humbert.    Eve Humbert.    Maria Daurignac

Police mugshots of the suspects under arrest.
*(Photo: © Jean-Loup Charmet, Paris).*

Humbert toys on sale in Paris.
*(Photo: © Mary Evans Picture Library, London)*

Le Petit Journal

Le Petit Journal          5 Centimes          SUPPLÉMENT ILLUSTRÉ          5 Centimes          ABONNEMENTS

Le Supplément illustré          Huit pages

L'ABONNEMENT MENSUEL, 5 cent.    —    La Mode in Petit Journal, 10 cent.

Quatorzième année          DIMANCHE 11 JANVIER 1903          Numéro 634

LA HAUTE PÈGRE
Arrivée de la famille Humbert à Paris

ARISTOCRATS OF CRIME: **The Humberts return to Paris.**

*(Photo: © Mary Evans Picture Library, London)*

Paris under police escort. "Give back the money, you old witch!" cried a workman watching Thérèse disembark, flanked by two detectives. The prisoners were locked up in separate cells in the Conciergerie (Thérèse's was opposite the cell that, just over a century earlier, had held Marie Antoinette).

Paris went wild with excitement that Christmas. People whistled ribald pop songs with titles like *The Humberts' Christmas*. Clockwork toys hawked on the streets included tiny Madame Humberts selling Spanish oranges, or escaping through the back windows of Spanish hideouts, pursued by the police with trails of banknotes fluttering behind. There was a Humbert board game, and a rubber balloon in the shape of a long thin Romain Daurignac who burst when you blew him up, deflating with a low moaning wail. Caricatures depicted the Humberts as a family theatrical troupe starring in melodramas called *Humbugs' Heritage* or *The Secrets of the Strongbox*. Sometimes they were a circus team or a conjuring act, with Thérèse strutting in the center as a whip-cracking ringmaster or wand-waving magician.

Interrogation of Madame Humbert.
*(Photo: © Mary Evans Picture Library, London)*

Madame Humbert takes command of the legal team.
*(Photo: © Topham Picturepoint)*

Something of this circus atmosphere carried over into the judicial interrogation in the new year of 1903. Top billing was reserved for a series of electric confrontations between the Humbert duo and the couple they had callously left to hold the bag for them, Monsieur and Madame Parayre. In the six months between the Humberts' disappearance and their arrest, "Parayre" had become a household word throughout France for infamy and shame. Lacking anyone else to blame, the press and public cast Armand Parayre as their scapegoat when the scandal first broke in May. His wife, who collapsed with misery and shock, was demonized in the popular prints as "the Cerberus of 65, avenue de la Grande Armée" or "Madame Humbert's evil genius." Policemen searched their apartment for incriminating evidence before sealing it, along with the rest of the Humberts' house. The hat shop belonging to their daughter, Amélie Matisse, was also raided. So was her husband's studio. The Parayres eventually fled Paris to take refuge in the tiny house of their younger daughter, Berthe, where detectives kept them under surveillance from a blind across the street.

Catherine Parayre confronting her
old friend and betrayer in court.
*(Photo: Alice Mackenzie)*

At Christmas 1902 Armand Parayre was arrested and imprisoned in a cell in the Conciergerie alongside the fugitives from Madrid. In January he was brought before the magistrate to face the Humberts for the first time since he had toasted the downfall of their enemies with them the previous May. Frédéric fainted under cross-examination, and had to be carried out of court. Thérèse flushed dark red when her former employee refused to take the hand she held out to him. Parayre's dignity and resolution impressed the magistrate, and calmed the spectators who had anticipated something more like a confrontation between snarling lions. On January 31, after six weeks in jail and a grueling public interrogation, he was set free and his name disappeared at last from the front pages of the newspapers.

❧

The proceedings continued to absorb the public all through the spring, with the trial itself promised for the summer. Observers compared the twists and turns of the dramatically unfolding plot to a

Captain Dreyfus's defense counsel, the great Maître Labori, center stage, with his clients Monsieur and Madame Humbert and Emile Daurignac in the dock behind him. *(Photo: © Jean-Loup Charmet, Paris)*

play, a novel in installments, or a serial thriller. All agreed that for pure inventiveness, the facts outstripped the wildest romantic fiction. Even her harshest critics conceded that Thérèse was beyond belief. F. I. Mouthon, whose investigative campaign had helped to precipitate her downfall, now found something Homeric about the sheer scale of operations that "raised burglary . . . to the height of a work of genius."

Thérèse herself rose to the occasion. At times she seemed positively to revel in it. In August 1903 she was finally brought to trial with her husband and two brothers (Maria Daurignac and Eve Humbert had been set free) before the Assize Court of the Seine. Fashionable Paris filled the courtroom. The solicitor general, Maître Blondel, opened for the prosecution, with Dreyfus's celebrated counsel, Maître Labori, retained by the defense. Thérèse faced a packed house with the masklike pallor and fiercely controlled energy of a great actress. "Beneath sharply incised brows, her great black eyes, dilated with battle fever, burned with a strange fire," wrote *Le Matin*'s Stéphane Lauzanne: "we were watching one of the most fantastic and one of the most gripping judicial spectacles it would be possible to see."

All eyes were riveted by Thérèse giving the last, in some ways the most dramatic, and certainly the most desolating performance of her life. Her voice regained its old mesmeric quality: husky, febrile, at times imperious but always with an

The international press reported a packed house in court for the last act of the Humbert Show. *(Photo: © Hulton Getty, London)*

undertone of pleading. People whom she had duped and exploited found they still could not entirely resist her spell. Maître Dumort of Rouen—who had lost his name, his reputation, and his law practice as well as every penny he possessed—confessed that he had been hypnotized. So did the distiller from Lille, Jean Schotmann, whose brother, Paul, had been shot when he refused the Humberts a second loan. Schotmann described how he had traveled up to Paris to see Madame Humbert after the murder, determined not to part with another *sou*, and found himself persuaded against his will not only to shell out a further two million francs, but to impersonate an imaginary Humbert uncle into the bargain. "I admit I was dumbfounded, but my surprise was so great that I did not protest. Since then I have come to realize that I was playing a part in a play, but I still can't explain how it happened."

Witness after witness testified to Thérèse's magic powers. People talked of her as a sorcerer or an enchantress ("With what composure she understood when to be vigilant, or haughty, or bewitching: how to tame and subjugate her subjects"). At one point a witness tried to assault Maître Labori. Cattaui's testimony degenerated into Punch-and-Judy name-calling, with cries of "Liar! Vampire! Wretch!" countered by: "Master blackmailer!" and "Crook!" During the prosecution's closing speech, Romain staged a nosebleed so copious that the courtroom had to be washed down. But few had eyes for anything save the spectacle of Thérèse as a hunted creature, trapped by the prosecutor's relentless exposure. "She experienced—and so did the public craning forward at the ringside to watch this unequal duel—the bitter and painful sensation that she was lost, that she was enclosed within a circle of fire drawing ever more tightly round her," wrote Lauzanne. "Until at last, definitively brought down, crushed on a scale beyond the dreams of her worst enemies, breathless and exhausted, like an animal captured and cowering on the ground, she almost fell into the arms of the warders who carried her out—as you might toss away a bundle of rags."

All observers agreed that Thérèse ended up as limp and woebegone as a deflated rubber toy. She and her husband were each sentenced to five years' solitary confinement with hard labor. Emile and Romain got two and three years respectively. None of the Humberts' lawyers ever practiced again, but no further charges were brought, and no attempt was made to look more closely at the web of corruption that had briefly been uncovered. The limited nature of the proceedings and the relative lightness of the sentences suggest that some sort of deal had been struck behind the scenes. If so, the Humberts kept their side of it. Thérèse served her sentence in the women's prison at Rennes. Frédéric served his at Melun, where he had once triumphed

Thérèse Humbert awaiting sentence in her cell in the Conciergerie. *(Photo: Alice Mackenzie)*

as a deputy. She was fifty-two years old and he was fifty-one when they were released. Nothing more was ever heard of either of them.

❧❧❧

**The Humbert affair** was barely mentioned again in history books, or personal memoirs. Those who suffered worst—top bankers, senior politicians, jurists like Du Buit, Jacquin, and Dumort who had believed in the Humberts to the end— had most to gain from keeping their humiliation quiet. Although Armand Parayre kept his nerve, his wife, Catherine, never recovered from the destruction of her faith in Thérèse, which was also her faith in herself. She lived just long enough to see her son-in-law, Henri Matisse, publicly reviled as a charlatan and confidence trickster. From 1905, on the strength of his showing at the Autumn Salon in Paris, Matisse was nicknamed "the Wild Beast" [or *le Fauve*] and his work was regularly dismissed by critics as an attempt to pull a fast one on the public. His wife, whose belief in him never wavered, repeated her mother's advice to pay no

La Grande Thérèse, stripped at last of all her trappings.
*(Photo: Alice Mackenzie)*

attention to the newspapers, but Catherine Parayre died in 1908, long before the world conceded that her son-in-law was a genuine magician after all.

A single observer in her lifetime attempted an aesthetic defense of Thérèse Humbert, arguing that hers was an imagination whose inventions sprang from the basic creative instinct to reshape experience. "If she had never left the South, none of this would have happened," wrote *Le Matin*'s columnist, H. Harduin:

> Madame Humbert was only trying to give herself a little of that illusion which is essential to cover up the miseries of existence, if you are poor. She thought she was at home, she didn't realize there would be people in the North stupid enough or credulous enough not to make allowances, not to take into account that element of fantasy, of imagination, without which reality seems too bare and harsh. . . . Madame Humbert forgot that what isn't necessarily true in the South is taken literally in the North, where you can't tell lies without being immediately believed.

Otherwise virtually no one had a good word to say for la Grande Thérèse, who had started out as a little girl telling fairy stories, and ended up being denounced by a procession of industrialists and bankers taking the witness stand in Paris, and

"Ah! poor Thérèse! You've gobbled up a hundred million, and now you'll have to gobble beans."

on the front pages of the national and international press. Some were contemptuous, others savagely angry. But many were not so much vindictive as rueful, incredulous, still half bewitched when they gave their evidence that August, rubbing their eyes and blinking, like people waking from a dream to find that their fairy gold had turned into dry leaves.

# Epilogue

I first came across la Grande Thérèse by chance seven years ago, in the course of research in and around Toulouse for a biography of Henri Matisse. Her story astounded me, and not simply because of the drastic impact her exposure—or rather the devastation it brought to his wife's family—had on Matisse's life. When I came to write the first volume of my biography, I had to fight so hard to relegate Thérèse to a minor role that, once it was finished, I felt I owed her a book of her own.

Having served her term of five years' hard labor, Thérèse vanished as completely as if she had never been. No one knows what happened after her release in 1908: where she lived, or how, or under what name, not even when and why she died. There were no interviews in her lifetime, and no obituaries to mark her end. It was admittedly not in the interest of the state to expose the Humberts to attention at a time when France had still not fully recovered from the Dreyfus scandal. Contemporaries freely admitted that, if the Dreyfus affair had knocked the stuffing out of the right wing and the army, the Humbert affair seemed likely to do the same for the left and its civil administration. The practical threat to the judiciary was compounded by the moral contamination that put the honor of the republic itself at stake. Prime Minister Waldeck-Rousseau was not alone in harboring grave misgivings about a criminal investigation almost certain to end up implicating one of his regime's founding fathers.

It was left to Waldeck-Rousseau's successor to preside over an exercise in damage limitation that has proved wholly successful from that day to this. Senator Humbert's involvement in the affair that bears his name has never before been closely examined (suggestive details previously ignored include, for instance, the fact that he was Thérèse's uncle by marriage as well as her father-in-law). His reputation remains intact in histories of the period, including the official *Dictionnaire de la biographie française* (on reaching *H* with its fifth and last volume in 1994). Thérèse herself is remembered dimly, if at all, as the heroine of a grotesquely comic episode briefly outlined in popular histories of great French fraudsters.

In 1993, when I crossed her tracks by accident while talking to local people in her native region, she seemed hardly definite enough to be a memory: more of a vague, capricious, insubstantial figment waiting in some transit lounge of limbo to be finally absorbed into folk myth. That first encounter sent me straight to the departmental reference library in Toulouse to find out more about her from newspaper reports and interviews published at the turn of the century. A friend who was with me ordered bound volumes of *Le Télégramme*, and I settled down with the city's famous radical organ, *La Dépêche*. We turned the pages with mounting incredulity.

❧❧❧

*La Grande Thérèse* may read like a fairy tale but I have invented nothing. The facts laid out here, together with every word of dialogue, come from contemporary sources. Toulouse's local press contains marvellously rich and detailed first-hand accounts of Thérèse's origins and character by people who had known her all her life. No one has ever drawn on them before. Previous versions of her story have been based almost exclusively on the Paris papers, which accurately reflect the widespread revulsion and contempt inspired by her downfall at the time. I have tried to trace Thérèse back to her beginnings, and to show her in her prime in the munificent Paris of the Belle Epoque when she and her family were far from the bedraggled fugitives who turned up in the dock in 1903 to be pelted with mud by all and sundry.

❧❧❧

There is some question as to whether Thérèse was her parents' firstborn child: one or two witnesses claimed her brother Emile as the elder of the two, other accounts suggest there may have been an even older sister (possibly fathered by Madame Daurignac's phantom Portuguese lover), who died young. Thérèse herself made much play with this alter ego, also called Thérèse, but the court ruled out her existence at the Humbert trial in 1903.

I would like to thank Marie-José Gransard for much help and guidance in the initial stages of research in 1993. My main sources have been the following newspapers during the period after the scandal broke (May–July 1902), the arrest and interrogation (December 1902-July 1903), and the trial itself (August 1903): *La Dépêche* and *Le Télégramme,* Toulouse; *Le Matin, Le Figaro,* and *La Gazette des Tribuneaux,* Paris; *Le Journal de Rouen* and *L'Indépendant de Cambrésis.*

Further accounts of the Humbert affair can be found in: *Thérèse Intime. Souvenirs de Mme. X* (anon., Paris, 1903); *La Vie à Paris* by Jules Claretie (Paris, 1904); *Notes sur la justice républi-caine,* by Henri Dutrait-Crozon (Paris, 1924); *La Belle Affaire* by H. Vonoven, Paris, 1925; *Famous*

*Crimes of Recent Times*, by Edgar Wallace, William Le Queux, et al. (London, n.d.); *Le Roman vrai de la 3e République,* vol. 1, *Prelude à la Belle Epoque,* ed. G. Guilleminault (Paris, 1956); and *Histoires d'Escrocs*, by Adam Pianko (Paris, 1997). The relevant chapter in *The Hypocrisy of Justice in the Belle Epoque,* by Benjamin F. Martin (Louisiana, 1984) is the only serious attempt I know of to investigate the political implications of the affair; and another previously unknown side effect is explored in my own *The Unknown Matisse: A Life of Henri Matisse, The Early Years, 1869–1908* (New York, 1998).

LE JEU DU LAPIN de la Grande Thérèse

mother visiting Graceland.

on her way to Hawaii.          Elvis took this—one of his favorites.

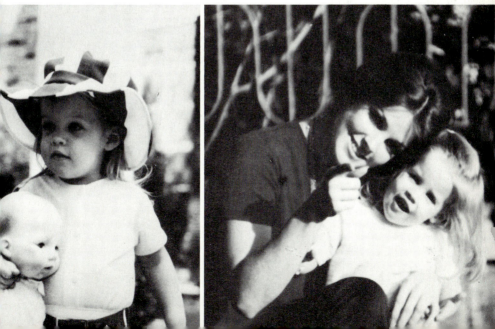

Lisa deciding whether to take a little ride on my custom chopper.

Lisa relaxing with friends, Snoopy and Brutus.

phis, 1971.
*ide World Photos*

Family picture.

Las Vegas, 1972.
*UPI/Bettmann Newsphotos*

Lisa and her daddy in Las Vegas on her birthday in 1973.

Vernon and Lisa, 1973.

Leaving Santa Monica Superior Court after the divorce, 1973.
*AP/Wide World Photos*

Four generations: (counterclockwise from top right) me, grandmother Lorana Iversen, my moth
Ann Beaulieu, my sister Michelle Beaulieu Hovey, Lisa.

Lisa, Grandma, and Delta at Graceland.

nd me clowning at Graceland.

Today.
*AP/Wide World Photos*

Today.
*Lorimar*

bed in the mornings as he gazed out at the gentle view of Rising Sun grazing in the pastures.

I thought of this ranch as a wonderful way for us to get away from Graceland from time to time. I pictured us saddling our own horses and riding in the early morning or at dusk. My picture was of us alone, without an entourage.

We were determined to buy it, never foreseeing the burden it would become. He wanted the ranch as much as I did, even though Vernon said that at $500,000 it was overpriced. He felt the owner could offer a much more desirable deal and tried to persuade us that financially it was not a good move. Elvis's movies were continuing to decline in popularity and record sales were down. He was averaging a million dollars a film and the money was going out as quickly as it was coming in. Yet Elvis's mind was made up. He wanted it.

Vernon grudgingly went to the bank to borrow money, putting Graceland up as collateral. We bought the entire ranch as was, including cattle and equipment, and christened it the Circle G for Graceland.

We had eighteen horses by then, and all were transferred to the ranch as was the staff of nine. It was the heyday of the commune, but Elvis had his own idea about how he wanted us all to live. Since the house on the property was small, he bought individualized mobile homes and designated one to each family. Vernon worked diligently to get permission from the city to put gas and water on the ranch.

"Whatever it takes, do it," Elvis ordered.

Before long, tons of cement were being poured to

make the huge concrete foundations for the trailers. It didn't stop there. He bought El Caminos or Ranchero trucks for each family, even one for the plumber and another for the painter. He spent at least $100,000 on trucks alone.

He continued spending money as if it were going out of style. Alarmed, Vernon literally begged him to stop, but Elvis said, "I'm having fun, Daddy, for the first time in ages. I've got a hobby, something I look forward to gettin' up in the mornin' for."

It wasn't unusual to see him walking around the property, knocking on doors, waking everyone up, or checking on the horses in the early-morning hours. He was having a ball, and there were days he didn't even want to take time out to eat—he'd walk around with a loaf of bread under his arm in case hunger pangs struck. He loved shopping in Sears's basement, buying power tools, knives, flashlights, and other equipment that he would come bearing proudly back to the ranch.

That spring of 1967, we spent a lot of time there, sometimes staying as long as two weeks without returning to Graceland. On Sundays we had picnics and all the girls chipped in on potluck, bringing chicken baskets, cookies, and salads. We rode horses, held skeet-shooting contests, and combed the lake for turtles and snakes. There was fun, laughter, and a lot of camaraderie. Once again, our life was a group affair with everyone participating.

Even in my tiny house there'd be guests for dinner every night, usually single guys like Lamar and Charlie. Cooking for Elvis was easy: I'd just take whatever we were having and burn it. But there were so many others that his cousin Patsy would usually stop by to help me. The guys with wives would have dinner in their mobile homes and then come over for dessert and spend the rest of the evening with us.

There was always a lot of jamming. Elvis, Lamar Fike, and Charlie Hodge would get together in the middle of the room, harmonizing a favorite song. When they were really going good Elvis would yell, "Whew! Hot damn! One more time!" He'd sometimes spend an hour just on an ending because it had "the *feel*—the ingredients of a masterpiece."

Just as the entourage had followed us to the ranch, so did the curious. The same ones who gathered around Graceland started turning up at the Circle G and soon— day or night—scores of people were lined up along the fence. Since our little house stood in full view of the road, Elvis built a ten-foot-high wall, but nothing deterred them; now they began climbing on tops of cars and roofs of nearby homes. We couldn't get away from them, and I dreaded driving through the gates.

The dream was slowly turning into a nightmare. The wives wanted to get back to their homes, and the children wanted to get back to their friends and their schools.

Elvis liked it when everyone was together—on terms he alone specified—and he got upset when they wanted to leave. "Hell, I bought all this stuff," he said, "and everyone wants to go home." He resented defections; he'd given the employees everything and they didn't seem to appreciate it. He discovered that some of the regulars were selling their trucks. They needed the cash more than the El Caminos. Elvis couldn't imagine the financial struggle most people face and he never understood that the married regulars had to consider responsibilities to their wives and children.

Still, he enjoyed giving and sharing even as his own bank account was radically diminishing. An expensive hobby, the ranch had already cost him close to a million dollars and created a serious cash-flow problem. In daily phone calls to the Colonel, Vernon pleaded with him to come up with some work to divert Elvis from his spending spree. The Colonel promptly made arrangements for another movie, *Clambake*. Elvis read the script, yet another beach-and-bikini story, and hated it. Vernon convinced him he didn't have much choice. "We need the money, Son." And Elvis was committed.

"I don't wanna leave here, Cilla," he said. "I don't want to leave you, the ranch, Sun. Ain't no son of a bitch gonna keep me away long. That goes for Daddy, Colonel, the studios—no one. Their little plot to keep me from spending money ain't gonna work. If I need money, I'll go to Nashville and record a few songs. It'll be better than those lousy goddamn pictures."

Neither he nor Vernon ever considered turning the Circle G into a profit-making operation. All the necessities for a successful farm were present—tractors, feed, and the finest Santa Gertrudis cattle, bred on the Rockefeller ranch—but he sold the cattle after Vernon advised him that upkeep was too expensive. With professional financial counsel, Elvis might have pursued legitimate business ventures beneficial to him and his hobby.

Unfortunately, Vernon and Elvis were leery of business matters requiring financial advice. Vernon operated on pure instinct, refusing any suggestion of tax breaks, which he found too complicated to consider. He let the IRS figure Elvis's taxes and had done so ever since Elvis had been audited while in the Army and assessed eighty thousand dollars in back taxes. "Let's just pay the taxes, Daddy," Elvis said. "I make enough money. I'll make a million dollars and I'll give them half."

It was during the filming of *Clambake* that our lease on the house on Perugia Way in Los Angeles expired and we had to go looking for a new home. After our experience at the Circle G, we were concerned with protecting our privacy, and when we spotted a secluded home nestled against a hill in Bel Air, we thought we'd found sanctuary at last. But privacy was to elude us here as well.

Soon, hundreds of people began collecting on the mountain road directly above us and observing the view below through binoculars and telephoto lenses. We could no longer use our pool, patio, or driveway without looking up at an audience, including reporters and photographers who were having a field day trying to get candid photos and scoops.

The situation occasionally got out of hand. One night when Elvis went to Mount Washington to talk with Daya Mata and I was driving to Joan Esposito's for a visit, I noticed a car with bright headlights tailgating me. It was one of Elvis's most ardent fans, a two-hundred-pound female who was accompanied by another girl and a guy. Feeling unsafe, I decided to turn around and go home. She followed close all the way and by the time I drove through the gates, I was furious.

Seeing her drive up to the dead-end road above our house, I sped after her, parking my car broadside across the road, blocking her. She was standing beside her car when I strode up and demanded: "What are you doing here? Why are you following me?" She stood there mutely and again I demanded: "Why are you following me?"

"You whore," she snapped.

Incensed, I clenched my fist and swung an uppercut, hitting her in the face. She landed on the ground, spread-eagled and stunned. I landed on her and the two of us yelled, screamed, and pulled hair until I realized I needed help. I ran back to our front gate and yelled into the intercom, "Someone—Sonny, Jerry—come help me!"

Within seconds Elvis came flying out of the house with the guys close behind him. "What is it, Baby?"

When I explained, pointing to the ridge, Elvis went charging up the hill. Seeing him coming, the girl and her friends locked themselves in her car. Elvis was livid, lifting the car on its springs, bouncing it from side to side. He pounded the windshield, threatening to kill them if he ever got his hands on them or if they ever laid their hands on me.

"I'm underage! I'm underage!" she kept yelling. "I'll sue you if you touch me."

It took a lot of convincing from Sonny that she was more trouble than it was worth before Elvis would let her drive away.

# 29

ELVIS WAS SO despondent over *Clambake* that his weight ballooned from his usual 170 to 200 pounds by the time he reported for work. The studio ordered him to take the weight off—and fast. Enter the diet pills, the only way he could curb his appetite and reduce his weight in the short time allowed. Colonel managed to deal with the impatient studio brass.

The morning he was to begin shooting he awoke groggy and went into the bathroom while I was still in bed. I heard a loud thump, then cursing. "Goddamn motherfucking cord! Who the hell put this thing here?"

I jumped out of bed and ran into the bathroom, calling out, "What's happened?" He was lying on the floor, rubbing his head.

"I tripped over the goddamn TV cord. It was so

damned dark in here I didn't see it. Help me out of here—I have to lie down."

Although he was dizzy and off balance, we managed to make it to the bed. Feeling a big lump on his head, I called Joe Esposito at once, who summoned Colonel Parker and a doctor. Within minutes, the room was full of people—the doctor, his nurse, Colonel Parker, and several nervous studio executives. Colonel suggested that everyone but himself wait outside while the doctor made his diagnosis.

A few hours later it was announced that Elvis had a severe brain concussion and that the start of his film would be delayed indefinitely. The Colonel decided to use the accident to curtail some of Elvis's other activities. He wanted Elvis to abandon his involvement with esoteric philosophies, which the Colonel felt were irrelevant to Elvis's acting career and detrimental to clear thinking.

Elvis's spiritual quest hadn't gone unnoticed. Everyone from the entourage to film crews was aware of a change in his personality over the years he'd studied with Larry Geller. Elvis's vibrant personality was now passive and he was becoming more introverted. The mischievous games he'd once played on movie sets had been superseded by studious pursuits. Elvis buried his head in books that he diligently lugged to and from the studio every day.

The person most concerned about this change was Colonel Parker. The Colonel felt that Larry'd hypnotized Elvis, and his acting and recording careers were suffering as a result. Elvis's "concussion" provided an opportunity to put a halt to the soul-searching.

A few days after the accident, the Colonel gathered Elvis and the boys together for a meeting and told them they were burdening Elvis with too many problems. "Dealing with one person is one thing," he said, "but eleven, plus his own problems, is enough for any man to buckle under."

The Colonel told them that there were going to be some changes, from cutting back the payroll to taking problems to Joe Esposito instead of Elvis. His basic message was: Leave Elvis alone.

"Elvis should concentrate on his career," he said. "He's an artist, not a shoulder to cry on. Leave him alone, and let him do his work." The Colonel looked over at Larry; it was obvious that his message was primarily aimed at him. "I don't want him reading any more books and getting involved in things that clutter up his mind."

Elvis sat and listened like an obedient child, looking down, saying nothing. He did not stand up for Larry; no one did.

Later the Colonel told Elvis that he should get Larry out of his life, that Larry used some sort of technique to manipulate his thinking. Elvis argued that this wasn't the case. He was truly interested in his readings.

"You wouldn't be in this condition if your head was on straight," shouted the Colonel. "I'm telling you, Larry's jamming up your mind."

I was surprised at how attentively Elvis was listening. Elvis had always argued with anyone, even me, who said anything against Larry. At one point, it seemed Elvis would cut off his right arm for Larry. But now Elvis promised the Colonel he wouldn't spend any more time than he had to with him. He kept his promise. He only used Larry to style his hair and was never alone with him again.

After that meeting, the boys became openly hostile toward Larry, and even Elvis began making a few pointed remarks about him. Larry was now the outsider, and he eventually left. Colonel Parker was elated. His boy was back.

Elvis was ready for a major change and it was time to move on. The Colonel said his films were doing badly and he had to revitalize his career. He'd be getting married soon, and before that date he'd have to get his career and life back on track.

After Larry left, Elvis locked away many of his books. I told him I was glad, that they were literally destroying us. We were engaged to be married. "Would it make you feel better if I just got rid of them all?" Elvis asked. I nodded.

That night, at three in the morning Elvis and I piled a huge stack of his books and magazines into a large box and dumped them into an abandoned water well behind Graceland. We poured gasoline over the pile, lit a match, and kissed the past goodbye.

# 30

MY ATTITUDE TOWARD the usual wedding formalities was naive and unsophisticated. If it had not been for my good friend Joan Esposito, I can't imagine what I would have done. Joanie was great that way. She was raised in Missouri, where her mother was somewhat involved with political events and ventures. Joanie knew all the social graces along with proper etiquette.

Before the wedding there had never been an occasion for formalities—the same people came around for years and were always included when there was a special party such as New Year's at a local club or fireworks wars in back of Graceland.

She reminded me to order my own personalized stationery for later thank-yous and a guest book for later memories. She registered our name with the city's finest silver and crystal dealers for the convenience of family and friends buying wedding presents.

I had never attended a wedding as large as ours—nothing even close. I was nervous. The bounty from the wedding showers took me by surprise. Graceland had always seemed to have everything anyone could want. We were content with what was there, plus little things I'd bought over the years, such as simple dishes and plain glasses (in case of breakage).

"What's wrong with those?" I wondered. I was raised to be practical and it was showing. Joanie introduced me to dining luxury, the top names in silver, crystal, china—Baccarat, Lenox, Steuben.

The wedding ceremony itself took place on May 1, 1967. Colonel Parker handled the arrangements. His plan was for Elvis and me to drive from L.A. to our rented house in Palm Springs the day before the wedding, so that any inquisitive reporters who got wind of the event would think it was going to take place there.

In fact, we planned to rise before dawn on our wedding day and fly from Palm Springs to Las Vegas, where we were scheduled to arrive at the city clerk's office at 7 A.M. to get our marriage license. From there, the plan was to rush over to the Aladdin Hotel, dress, have a small ceremony in the private suite of the hotel's owner, and then—we hoped—slip out of town before anyone noticed.

Time was of the essence. We knew that once we applied for a marriage license, the news would flash around the world. It actually was only a few hours after we got our license that Rona Barrett's office began calling to ask if rumors about the marriage were true.

Elvis and I followed the Colonel's plan, but as we raced through the day we both thought that if we had it to do over again, we would have given ourselves more time. We were particularly upset at the way our friends and relatives ended up being shuffled around. The Colonel even told some of the boys that the room was too small to hold most of them and their wives, and that there wasn't time to change to a bigger room. Unfortunately, by the time Elvis found out, it was too late for him to do anything about it.

Now I sometimes look back at all the commotion of that week and wonder how things could have gotten so out of hand. I wish I'd had the strength then to say, "Wait a minute, this is *our* wedding, fans or no fans, press or no press. Let us invite whomever we want, and have it wherever we want!"

It seemed that as soon as the ceremony began, it was over. Our vows were taken. We were now husband and wife. I remember flashbulbs popping, my father's congratulations, my mother's tears of happiness.

I would have given anything for one moment alone with my husband. But we were immediately rushed out for a photo session, then a nationwide press conference, and finally a reception, with more photographers.

Mrs. Elvis Presley. It had a different ring, a nicer sound than previous labels such as "constant companion," "teen heartthrob," "live-in Lolita," "lover." For the first time, I felt accepted by my peers and the majority of the public. There were exceptions, of course—those who had that little hope that they might be the one to finally catch Elvis. I didn't understand that at the time. I was in love and just hoped they would be happy for us.

When I read in the newspapers that I was the best-kept secret in Hollywood, I felt very proud; it was good to be acknowledged. The years of doubt and insecurity of where and if I belonged were over.

I was both exhausted and relieved when we finally returned to Palm Springs aboard Frank Sinatra's Learjet, the *Christina*. There were more photographers and reporters waiting for us as we stepped off the plane, and others were parked outside our home.

I was surprised that Elvis was holding up so well, considering how nervous he'd been about this ultimate commitment. Yet he was charming with the press and dealt easily with endlessly clicking cameras and flashbulbs, all of which he could usually tolerate only for short periods of time. On top of everything else, we hadn't slept for nearly forty-eight hours.

In his own way, Elvis was determined that our wedding day would be special for us. He joked with Joe Esposito, asking, "Is this the way it's done?"

He carried me across the threshold of our house singing "The Hawaiian Wedding Song. He stopped and gave me a long, loving kiss, then proceeded to carry me up the stairs to our bedroom, the whole crowd teasing and applauding.

It was still daylight and the sun shone brightly through our bedroom windows as Elvis carefully placed me in the middle of our king-size bed.

I don't think he really knew what to do with me. After all, Elvis had protected me and saved me for so long. He was now understandably hesitant about fulfilling all his promises about how very good this moment was going to be.

Looking back, I have to laugh when I remember how nervous we both were. One would have thought that it was the first time we had ever been together under intimate circumstances.

Gently, his lips touched mine. Then he looked deeply into my eyes. "My wife," he said softly, as he drew me close. "I love you, Cilla," he murmured, covering my body with his.

The intensity of emotion I was experiencing was electrifying. The desire and lust that had built up in me throughout the years exploded in a frenzy of passion.

Could he have known how it would be for me? Had he planned this all along? I'll never know. But I do know that as I went from child to woman, the long, romantic, yet frustrating adventure that Elvis and I had shared all seemed worthwhile. As old-fashioned as it might sound, we were now one. It was special. *He* made it special, like he did with anything he took pride in.

# 31

WITHIN A FEW DAYS we were in Memphis, where Dee Presley held a small wedding shower for me. At the end of May we threw a big reception at Graceland for all *our* friends and relatives—and some fans. Elvis and I wore our wedding clothes, greeted everyone, sipped champagne, and shared cake just as if the party were taking place after the wedding ceremony. It was much more comfortable and relaxed than Las Vegas.

Laughing and somewhat high from the champagne, we could really have a good time. There were no photographers or strangers watching our every move.

It was fun seeing Vernon get loose.

"Daddy, you want some more champagne?" Elvis asked, his eyes twinkling.

"Don't mind if I do, Son. That's pretty good stuff."

"Yeah. Well, don't drink too much. I don't want my daddy gettin' in trouble. I see that blonde you've been eyein'."

Vernon stole a glance at the girl and, with the same twinkle replied, "She ain't too bad, is she? Think I'll go see if she needs anything."

Elvis turned to me and said, "I like seein' Daddy happy. He hasn't had too much of it lately, poor ol' guy." He watched Vernon make his way through the crowd.

The reception at Graceland was our way of trying to make everyone happy—those who hadn't known about the wedding ceremony, those who knew but couldn't attend, and those who knew but weren't invited. It was a way of including everyone, of making up to anyone whose feelings might have been hurt during the rushed hours in Vegas.

One person who had been very upset was Red West. He had not been invited to the wedding ceremony in the suite, only to the reception afterward. I believe the reason Red was so hurt was because Elvis did not demand that he be present, did not take a stand over Colonel Parker's decision that only the immediate family and best man attend. I also believe that Red wanted to be best man. After all, he'd known Elvis the longest, since their days at Humes High. When Red found out he could not watch the ceremony, he refused to come at all.

Elvis was aware of Red's decision but was determined not to let anything mar the wedding. I understood that but was never able to figure out how Marty Lacker made it to the ceremony. In a last-minute decision Elvis had included him as best man along with Joe Esposito.

It took a long time for Red to come around again without showing his displeasure. This bothered Elvis and he discussed it with many of us, justifying himself and blaming Colonel for putting him in an awkward position.

"You didn't make the decision—I did," Colonel reportedly stated. "No matter who you picked, there was gonna be someone left mad. You got too many as it is. You oughta listen to me and let go of some of 'em, then these things won't come up."

There's an old Southern belief that holds that a woman goes into a marriage thinking she can change her man, while a man wants his woman to stay the same as when he married her. I didn't want to change Elvis, but I did have the romantic delusion that once we were married, I could change our life-style.

For the first few days after the wedding, I thought my dream had come true. We divided our time between Graceland and the ranch, where Elvis and I had taken up residence in a large, three-bedroom trailer.

It was typical of Elvis to choose the trailer over the quaint little house. He had never lived in a trailer before and it intrigued him. The place was completely furnished, including a washer, a dryer, and a modern kitchen. It turned out to be very romantic.

I loved playing house. I personally washed all his clothes, along with the towels and sheets, and took pride in ironing his shirts and rolling up his socks the way my mother had taught me. Here was an opportunity to take care of him myself. No maids or housekeepers to pamper us. No large rooms to embrace the regular entourage.

I got up early, put on a pot of coffee, and started his breakfast with a pound of bacon and three eggs, proudly presented it to him the moment he woke up.

"You see, if we were ever stranded somewhere alone, you know I can take care of you."

It must have been difficult for him to eat the instant he opened his eyes—but he wasn't going to disappoint his new bride.

Although the rest of the group traveled with us, they respected our privacy as newlyweds and, for the most part, left us alone.

I understood Elvis's need for the camaraderie the entourage provided, and I didn't want to take him away from the people he loved, especially now that we were married. He had always criticized wives who tried to change the status quo. He told me about one wife, saying, "She doesn't like him to be around the boys so much. She's going to cause problems in the group." The last thing I wanted was for Elvis to think I'd be the kind of wife who'd come between her man and his friends.

I decided one evening to show off my cooking skills for everyone by making one of Elvis's favorite dishes, lasagna. I invited the regulars, bragging to one and all about how well I prepared this Italian specialty. Despite my outward confidence, I must have made ten long-distance calls to my mother in New Jersey, checking and rechecking on quantities and measurements. It was important for me to prove myself a success. Joe Esposito, our only Italian and a "gourmet chef," kidded me all week about how he bet that my lasagna wouldn't be as good as his. All that ribbing only made me more nervous. I kept thinking, What do I know about pasta? I'm not even Italian.

Finally, the night of the dinner came. Everyone was seated at the table, watching me expectantly. I tried to appear cool and confident as I brought out the fancily prepared platter and started cutting individual squares for my guests. I did notice that when I started slicing the lasagna, it felt a little tough, but thinking I was holding a dull knife, I continued dishing it out.

I sat down, smiled anxiously, and said, "Please start." We all took a bite and—crunch. There was a look of shock on everyone's face. I looked at my plate and was mortified when I realized I had forgotten to boil the pasta.

Elvis began laughing, but when he saw I was about to cry he turned to his plate and began eating, uncooked noodles and all. Taking their lead from him, everyone followed suit.

Joe Esposito still laughs about it, frequently saying, "Cilla? How about some lasagna?"

# 32

───────── ∾ ─────────

ELVIS AND I often talked of having children, but we certainly weren't planning on having them right away. Then one day we were at the ranch. It was early afternoon and Elvis was still asleep. I lay in bed and felt a strange sensation in my stomach, a sensation I'd never felt before. I lay staring at the ceiling. No—it couldn't be. Again, the same feeling. I slid out of bed. I'll call Patsy, I thought. She'd know. I went to the phone in the next room.

"Patsy, when you found out you were pregnant, did you feel strange?"

"Strange like what?"

"You know. I mean, what did you feel?"

"Well, I missed my period."

"But didn't you feel something in your body, something strange?"

"I really don't remember, Priscilla. Why?"

"Because I think I'm pregnant. I know I am. I've never felt this before."

"Maybe it's nerves."

"No—I just have a funny feeling. I'll talk to you later."

I didn't tell Elvis right away: I couldn't. But he saw that I was quiet and preoccupied.

If I were pregnant, I knew that our plans to travel would have to be postponed. I wouldn't be able to head off to some exotic locale and leave my child with nurses and maids. For the first year, I truly wanted to be alone with Elvis, without any responsibilities or obligations.

For a few days I was angry with Elvis. Before the wedding I asked him if I should start taking birth-control pills, but he had been adamantly against it.

"They're not good for you. I really don't want you taking them. They're not perfected yet, Baby. There's all kinds of side effects."

A week passed before I told Elvis my suspicions. I expected him to react with the same mixed emotions I'd felt, but he was ecstatic. He made arrangements for me to see a doctor right away, accompanied me to the doctor's office, and sat anxiously in the waiting room while I was examined.

When I came out I put my arms around him and said, "Guess what?"

"What? What?" He was barely able to contain himself.

"You're going to be a daddy."

He couldn't believe it and immediately wanted to tell everyone. Just then his father, who had driven over with us, came into the room. Elvis grabbed him.

"Daddy, you won't believe this. Cilla's gonna have a baby. You're gonna be a granddaddy."

"Good Lord Almighty," Vernon said, stunned. "You're kiddin' me."

"No, Daddy. We're telling you the truth." Then Elvis teased him, saying, "You're going to be a gray-headed granddaddy."

I loved seeing Elvis happy, but I was still uncertain about how my unexpected pregnancy would affect our marriage. This was supposed to have been our time alone. I wanted to be beautiful for him; instead, my debut as Elvis's bride was going to be spoiled by a fat stomach, puffy face, and swollen feet.

As far as I was concerned, the less people mentioned about my looking pregnant, the better. I intended to prove that a pregnant woman did not have to get fat. I wanted to refute Elvis's claim that "women use the excuse of their pregnancy to let themselves go." Although the doctor said that a twenty-five-pound gain would be fine, I immediately dropped from my normal one hundred ten pounds to one hundred. During the next four months, I regained just five pounds, and only nine more by the time of delivery. Eating one meal a day and snacking on apples and hard-boiled eggs, I prided myself on never needing to buy a maternity outfit. My doctor advised that in addition to taking multiple vitamins I should consume plenty of dairy products. Being vain, I amended my doctor's instructions and lessened my intake of dairy products. I did not want to gain weight and get stretch marks. As a further precaution I resolved to slather myself with cocoa butter for the next eight months.

A few days after I learned I was pregnant, we left Memphis for L.A., where Elvis was to begin preproduction on a new film, *Speedway.* It was to be the last drive in our customized bus before it was sold. During the trip, Elvis and the guys had a ball, punching each other and playing practical jokes. I played photographer, clicking away at everyone. But when I kept smiling and laughing I still felt very ambivalent about my pregnancy. I wanted a baby, just not so soon.

Elvis was extremely sensitive to my moods. He missed his little girl's "twinkling eyes," her "bright, smiling face." Finally, in Flagstaff, Arizona, at a small roadside inn, he sat me down and said, "What do you want to do, Little One?"

I broke down and answered, "I don't know. What can I do?"

"What do you think?" he said. "I'll back you up whatever you want to do."

Instantly I knew what he was talking about. He was leaving the decision up to me. "It's our baby," I said, sobbing. "I could never live with myself, neither could you."

There were no words, only his smile of approval; he held me tightly in his arms as I cried. The two of us, bound by love, accepted our new little creation wholeheartedly.

# 33

WHEN I FIRST felt my baby move I suddenly understood the full joy of carrying our child. My smile returned when Elvis delicately placed his hand on my slightly swollen stomach and said, "How can such a little creature carry another little young'un?" The pregnancy was bringing us closer. He would call me from the studio every day, just to say hello and make sure I was fine. It was because of the baby that we decided to buy our first home in Los Angeles instead of leasing as we'd done in the past. While he was filming I searched the Beverly Hills–Bel Air area for a place that would suit us.

Later that fall, when we were in Arizona for location filming on *Stay Away, Joe*, I saw an advertisement in *Variety* for a house that sounded perfect: a beautiful home in Trousdale Estates, completely furnished, three bedrooms, a guest cottage, pool, and good security.

PRISCILLA BEAULIEU PRESLEY

I flew back to L.A. The house was owned by a prominent landowner who was recently divorced. With a built-in bar, antique furnishings, and collectors' art, it was a far cry from Rocca Place, where each room was decorated to each employee's specification—a different carpet, a different color, a different style in each room. Unfortunately, I'd tried to satisfy everyone's taste, and architectural indigestion was the result. This time I would be able to live with everything the way I liked.

As soon as Elvis returned from Arizona we moved into our new home and began preparing a room for our baby. All I could think about was how happy I was, how wonderful life was.

Naturally, I got a lot of advice about what I should and shouldn't do while I was pregnant. Steeped in her Southern superstitions, Grandma was especially solicitous, telling me I couldn't brush my hair over my head or else I would wrap the umbilical cord around the baby. She also said I shouldn't stand on my feet too long or my legs would swell and I wouldn't be able to walk again. She was as concerned as any doting mother and some of my activities gave her reason to worry. I still kept up with my ballet, rode my motorcycle and my horse Domino, right up until the eighth month of pregnancy. Elvis thought I was absolutely incredible to keep up with him in every way. That made me happy. I was pleasing him and still by his side every day.

Then I began hearing rumors about Elvis and Nancy Sinatra, the same rumors that I had read about in Germany: that she had a passionate crush on him, that they were having an affair. I was extremely sensitive and quick to cry. Elvis assured me that I was just being over-sensitive because of my condition. I agreed. Six months into my pregnancy Nancy called and said she'd like to give me a baby shower. I didn't know her that well and thought it a little strange that she was so accommodating. But Elvis assured me that she was very nice and that I should get to know her. It was agreed that I would go to the shower under one condition, which Colonel suggested: All the pictures that were taken that day were to be handed over to me. That way, there'd be no shots popping up in the national movie magazines. It turned out quite nicely. Nancy was very friendly and very supportive. I found that I liked her and I decided to ignore the rumors.

Life takes such surprising turns. Just when you're getting confident, along comes the unexpected. I was upstairs at Graceland when Elvis called me to his office, the one adjoining my dressing room. "Cilla, I have to have time to think. Things just aren't going right. It'll be good for the two of us to take a little time off, like a trial separation. Be apart from one another for a while."

I wanted to die. I was seven months along and could not believe what I was hearing. It had to be a joke. "What are you saying? What did I do?"

"You didn't do anything, Baby. You don't understand. It's not you. It's just that I'm going through some things. I think it'd be better if we took a little break."

I looked at him in silence, feeling a new strength. If he excluded me at this time, then he didn't deserve me at all. I stood up and said, "You've got it. Just tell me when to leave." I went into my dressing room and closed the door.

I was numb. This was not the man I knew. I instinctively withdrew, my affection numbed, my thoughts suspicious, my heart aching.

I don't think Elvis really intended to leave me. It wasn't his style. I later realized he too had questions about how a baby would affect his life. Would his public accept him as a father? He wasn't even sure if his fans had adapted to his becoming a husband. How loyal would they be?

Within a short time Elvis's sensitive nature brought him back to his senses. Two days had passed. The idea of a trial separation was never mentioned again. We both acted as if nothing had been said. It was at times like this that I wished Elvis and I had the ability to truly communicate with each other, to confront our insecurities, fears, and frustrations instead of pretending these feelings weren't there. We probably would have been surprised at how much understanding we both really had. I could not escape the impact his words had on me, leaving me with a sense of doubt.

As my pregnancy progressed, we still played hard. I wanted to be included in everything that everyone else did. That Christmas we went to the ranch and rode horses, had snowball fights and went on hayrides. Elvis would sit up front in the wagon and call out to me, "How you doing, Cilla? That's my girl. How's she doing back there?"

I'd call back, "She's doing pretty good. I'm okay."

If we'd go horseback riding, he'd always ask me, "Are

you sure you can do this? Did the doctor say you could?"

"Yes," I'd answer. "I can do it."

I was determined not to ask for special treatment.

It was only in the last month or so that I slowed down at all. Instead of sitting through two or three films a night, Elvis would take me home after just one.

He arranged his schedule so that he could be home with me at Graceland during the final month. To be absolutely prepared for the big day, we even performed practice drills for the trip to Baptist Memorial Hospital. As my time drew near, Elvis became more and more nervous.

On February 1, 1968, I awoke about eight o'clock and found the bed beneath me soaking wet. Frightened, I called my mother in New Jersey and she suggested I ring the doctor immediately. He told me to head straight for the hospital. I gently woke Elvis up and told him the big day had arrived. Elvis groggily asked me if I was sure. When I said yes, he called Vernon and told him to notify everyone, then yelled downstairs, "She's ready! Cilla's going to have the baby!"

Ignoring his frenzy, I disappeared calmly into the bathroom and applied my ever-so-black mascara and teased my ever-so-black hair. Later at the hospital I requested special permission to keep on my double set of lashes.

Downstairs there was pandemonium. As planned, the decoy cars raced off first, Lamar and Joe frantically waving for the fans to follow them. Then we took off, but despite the rehearsals we headed straight for the wrong hospital. We had changed hospitals, but obviously Jerry, who was driving, hadn't been informed. Charlie Hodge saved the day, convincing Jerry it was Baptist Memorial, not Methodist. Luckily we arrived in time.

Our daughter, Lisa Marie, was born at 5:01 that afternoon. The nurse brought her into my room and I cradled her in my arms. I couldn't believe she was mine, that I had borne this child. She was so tiny, so beautiful. Elvis came into the room and kissed me, thrilled that we had a perfectly normal, healthy baby. He was already in love with her. He watched me holding her and his eyes misted with happiness. Then he took us both in his arms and held us.

"Nungen," he whispered, which was his way of saying "young one." "Us has a little baby girl."

"Her knows," I whispered back.

I asked if he wanted to hold her. He looked petrified at first, but then he started to touch her. He played with her hands, her feet. He was in awe, saying, "I can't believe that I made part of this beautiful child." Elvis knew that I had wanted the baby to have dark hair like his, and Lisa had been born with lots of silky black hair. "She's so perfect," he said, "even the color of her hair is right."

We stayed in each other's arms for a long time, caressing our infant and each other, a young couple sharing the first pleasures of parenthood.

The man in my hospital room that day was the man I loved, and will always love. He didn't have to try to be strong and decisive or sexy, he wasn't afraid to show his warmth or vulnerability. He didn't have to act the part of Elvis Presley, superstar. He was just a man, my husband.

# 34

IN MY DIARY entry dated April 5, I wrote, "The baby's getting more beautiful as each day goes by. Dr. Turman said she's healthy and progressing well. Elvis went with me to the pediatrician, waiting outside in the car. He also accompanied me to the obstetrician. He's insisting I keep up with my regular checkups—taking care of both of us like a doting father.

"But I've been lonely for him since the baby's birth; he is still withdrawn. It's been two months and he still hasn't touched me. I'm getting concerned."

The following day, I wrote, "I asked Elvis if anything was wrong, if he's lost his desire for me. I saw this made him a little uncomfortable. He told me he wants to make sure my system's back to normal—that he doesn't want to hurt me. That made me feel a little better.

"We brought Lisa to our room, put her in the middle of the bed with us. She's such a good baby—we can't believe she's ours."

Elvis and I started getting back into our regular routine. Since the baby was born, we were spending more time at Graceland, eventually moving all the horses back to the original stables, Vernon selling much of the equipment and, later, the Circle G itself.

Elvis accepted fatherhood with a great deal of joy, but the fact that I was a mother had a disquieting effect on him. I didn't understand at the time, but later on I would learn more about men who are very close to their own mothers. I am no purveyor of Freudian theory. I believe when a man comes into the world, his first unconditional love is his mother. She cuddles him, gives him warmth, the breast for nourishment, and everything he needs to exist. None of those feelings has a sexual connotation. Later, when his own wife becomes a mother, this bank of memories is ripped open and his passion may dissipate.

When Elvis's mother was alive they had been unusually close. Elvis even told her about his amatory adventures, and many nights when she was ill, he would sleep with her. All the girls he took out seriously had to fulfill Gladys's requirements of the ideal woman. And as with me, Elvis then put the girl on a pedestal, "saving her" until the time was sacred and right. He had his wild times, his flings, but any girl he came home to he had to respect.

Now I was a mother and he was uncertain how to treat me. He had mentioned before we were married that he had never been able to make love to a woman who'd had a child. But throughout my pregnancy—until the last six weeks—we had made love passionately. He'd been very careful each time, afraid that he might hurt the baby or me, but he was always loving and sensitive to my needs. Now months had passed.

On April 20 I wrote in my diary: "I embarrassed my-self last night. I wore a black negligee, laid as close to Elvis as I could while he read. I guess it was because I knew what I wanted and was making it obvious. I kissed his hand, then each finger, then his neck and face. But I waited too long. His sleeping pills had taken effect. An-other lonely night."

Finally, months later Elvis made love to me. Before we made love, he told me I was a young mother now, that being the mother of his child is very special. But I wrote in my diary, "I am beginning to doubt my own sexuality as a woman. My physical and emotional needs were un-fulfilled."

# 35

WE RETURNED to Los Angeles, where Elvis was filming *Live a Little, Love a Little*. He started getting into his old habits again. Frustrated, I started searching for dance classes to enroll in. I looked through the local Yellow Pages until one class caught my attention, a school for jazz and ballet not far from home.

The studio was small and unpretentious; the owner, Mark, was an extremely attractive and dynamic man of forty-five. He was an excellent dancer and a fine teacher, and by the time I left that afternoon, I had enrolled for private lessons.

Still too shy to dance in front of a group, I wanted to wait until I was sure I could keep up with the other dancers before taking a class. I began taking private lessons three times a week. Mark's personal interest and attention were flattering, and I was soon doing lifts and jumps, things I'd never thought I could accomplish.

He said I had the potential to be a good dancer, and he pushed me to the limit. Out of frustration and pain I would want to quit. Demanding that I continue, he told me I was building character and forced me to repeat the same routine until it was nearly perfected. This made me realize that I could go further than I'd ever dreamed.

He believed in me, and I was accomplishing something. For the first time I was creating, feeling good about myself, and I couldn't wait to get to class each day.

Mark was charismatic and I was particularly vulnerable. In lieu of a passionate marriage, dance was becoming my life; I was obsessed with it, taking all my frustrations and feelings into the studio. I found myself thinking about Mark even when I was home. I had only seen him a few times in my life and yet I was unable to get him out of my mind. I rationalized, telling myself it was because he was always *there* for me. He seemed to understand me, while the man I truly loved was involved in his own world. I began to relax, enjoying myself almost against my will. It had been a while since I'd spent some time with a man who validated my abilities and appreciated spending time with me alone. It was also the first time I was not competing for my own identity. This was a high I had not experienced recently. I had a brief affair and decided to end it.

I came out of it realizing I needed much more out of my relationship with Elvis. Elvis and I decided to get away to Hawaii.

This was the first time we'd gone on holiday, and I

was hoping that it would be a second honeymoon, that my experience with Mark would be forgotten. We took along Lisa, her nurse, Joe, Joanie, Patsy and her husband, Gee Gee, Lamar and his wife Nora, and Charlie. We checked into the Ilikai Hotel on Waikiki, but soon found that Elvis couldn't go to the beach without attracting a crowd. We decided to rent a house on a private beach and spent the rest of our vacation there.

We had a great time, and Elvis and I were like two kids again, away from the pressures and the filming—and away from Mark, to whom my attention would occasionally wander.

It was there that we met Tom Jones, and Elvis became very fond of him. He had always enjoyed Tom's vocal style, especially in "Green, Green Grass of Home," which Elvis had first heard while traveling from L.A. to Memphis. He'd called me when they'd stopped in Arizona, encouraging me to get the record.

Elvis was positive Tom was black; no white singers could belt out a song like that, except the Righteous Brothers, who much to his surprise were also white.

Tom Jones and Elvis enjoyed an instant rapport. After an appearance at the Ilikai, Tom invited us to his suite, along with our group. Within minutes the champagne exploded and the party was on. We laughed, drank, joked, drank some more (lots more), jammed—and reeled back to the Ilikai at dawn. Elvis had had such a good time he personally invited Tom and his group to join us the next day at our beach house. A friendship was born, a friendship of mutual respect and admiration.

One of Elvis's outstanding attributes was his conviction that there was room for anyone with talent in the entertainment field. In my experience, only a few stars are this generous. Greed, insecurity, jealousy, ego usually keep celebrities from supporting one another.

Elvis could spot talent instantly. In Las Vegas, we regularly took in lounge acts featuring various up-and-coming artists, and if Elvis liked the show, he patronized the club, encouraging the entertainers to pursue their careers, infusing them with confidence and enthusiasm.

Some of his favorites were Ike and Tina Turner, Gary Puckett and the Union Gap, dancers Tybe and Bracia, and old-timers Fats Domino and the Ink Spots, all talented people deserving acknowledgment in their craft.

One night we visited Barbra Streisand backstage at the International Hotel, now the Hilton. It was a classic Streisand performance and Elvis, after a few too many Bloody Marys, wanted to tell Barbra his impressions. We were ushered backstage to her dressing room and Elvis's first words upon meeting her were: "What did you ever see in Elliott Gould? I never could stand him."

In typical Streisandese she retorted, "Whaddya mean? He's the fah-tha of my child!"—leaving Elvis speechless.

Elvis had some other very special favorites—Arthur Prysock, John Gary, opera star Robert Merrill, Brook Benton, Roy Orbison, and Charles Boyer's recording "Where Has Love Gone?"

He couldn't abide singers who were, in his words, "all technique and no emotional feeling" and in this category he firmly placed Mel Torme and Robert Goulet. They were both responsible for two television sets being blown away with a .357 Magnum.

# 36

ELVIS'S FIVE-YEAR contract with MGM was up in 1968 and he was finally free to move on to new challenges. Even Colonel admitted that Elvis's career needed a shot in the arm. NBC made him an offer to do his own television special, with newcomer Steve Binder directing. There was no initial format, but the idea was tempting and the money was right. The fact that there was no script—that it was an "open development"—made Colonel hesitant to agree. Colonel demanded more control than that, but Elvis wanted to meet Steve, make sure that they could get along, speak the same language.

It had been years since Elvis had appeared on TV and he was nervous. To his surprise, Steve was much younger than he had anticipated, extremely perceptive, and soft-spoken, a startling contrast to the studio heads he'd

worked with, men much older, with hardened, precon-
ceived opinions on how Elvis should be packaged and
sold. For the first time in years he felt creative. Steve
Binder gained Elvis's trust and had the sensitivity to let
Elvis just be Elvis. Steve observed, took mental notes,
learned Elvis's ways, discovered what made his star
comfortable and what got him uptight.

During their meetings Steve sensed Elvis's fear that he
hadn't been before a live audience in years but he noticed that Elvis came alive backstage in the dressing
room jamming with the musicians.

Each day he grew more confident and excited about
his new project, taking pride once again in his appearance, watching his weight, following his diet, and working closely with the show's costume designer, Bill Belew,
creating a look we hadn't seen him sport in years—the
black leather suit.

I was surprised when he said, "Sattnin, I feel a little
silly in that outfit. You think it's okay?"

Elvis knew this special was a big step in his career. He
could not fail. For two straight months he worked harder
than on all his movies combined. It was the most important event in his life.

During this time I was discovering whole new worlds
of music—Segovia; Blood, Sweat and Tears; Tchai-
kovsky; Santana; Mason Williams; Ravel; Sergio

Mendes; Herb Alpert—and I was anxious to share my new enthusiasms, music and dance, with my husband. I wanted to bring energy to our relationship in the hope of strengthening our marriage. Discussions at the dinner table now included Leonard Bernstein and Carlos Montoya, but they held no appeal for Elvis; the TV special was consuming all his thoughts.

He was away much of the time, and when we did see each other our level of communication was strictly superficial. Each absorbed in our own separate pursuits, we had little in common except our daughter. My approach with him was delicate: I was aware of the distance growing between us. But because of his preoccupation with the special, I realized that the last thing he needed from me was a statement that I feared we were drifting apart.

In his absence, I was taking care of Lisa in addition to attending dance classes in the morning, ballet in the early evening, and two jazz classes at night, lasting often until one in the morning. I was now studying with a new dance instructor, who was using me to give demonstrations for the evening classes. Many of the students were professional dancers. I had diligently worked my way into the company, rehearsing four hours every day to master new steps, constantly pushing myself to new limits, and eventually I was to take a place in the dance company, anonymously performing shows on weekends at colleges in the L.A. area.

Elvis's Singer TV special was a huge success, the highest-rated special of the year, and his finale, "If I Can Dream," was his first million-selling record in years. We

sat around the TV watching the show, nervously antici-
pating the response. Elvis was quiet and tense through
the whole program, but as soon as the calls started, we all
knew he had a new triumph. He hadn't lost his touch.
He was still the King of Rock and Roll.

It was a blessing for both of us. The hours I devoted to
dance released him from the strain of my dependence.
My new interest didn't pose a threat in the sense that
taking up a profession would have. I was still there to
tend to his needs, as he wanted his wife to be, while also
creating my own world, no longer intimidated by the
magnitude of his. I was growing, learning, and expand-
ing as an individual.

This new freedom nearly came to an abrupt end when
a newcomer to the clan decided to take it upon himself to
investigate my comings and goings. He reported to Elvis
that I was seen coming out of a dance studio at a late
hour and did Elvis want him to carry it any further.
Elvis's unpredictability in dealing with certain crises in
life could be astounding. Logically, such a volatile man
would explode. Instead, he made no accusations. His
only comment was, "Little One, there are some people
who are insinuating you've been seen coming out of a
dance studio at late hours."

"It's true. You know I'm part of the company. It's not
just me leaving. That's the time we break."

I pleaded with him to tell me who was starting trouble. All he would say was, "Let's put it this way: He's
new and he's treading on dangerous ground. If he knows
what's good for him, he better keep the fuck to his own
business."

After the success of his special, Elvis devoted several weeks to a recording session, and again he was highly motivated. For the first time in fourteen years, he'd been persuaded to record in Memphis, at the American Sound Studios, a black company where major artists, including Aretha Franklin, had recorded their most recent hits. The studio musicians were young and Elvis had a great rapport with them. More importantly, he made great music with them.

He'd be at the studio singing until the early-morning hours and then return the next evening, full of energy and ready to start again. His voice was in top form and his excitement was infectious. Each cut was more terrific than the one before. We'd listen to the songs over and over, Elvis yelling, "All right, listen to that sound," or "Goddamn, play it again."

Colonel stayed away from this session. Elvis was the artist, and he was on a roll. He ended up recording so many songs, it took RCA a year and a half to release them all, including hits like "In the Ghetto," "Kentucky Rain," and "Suspicious Minds."

Watching Elvis sing with confidence again, honing each word in his own style, filled us all with pride. What a contrast to sessions in the past that had been filled with anger, frustration, and disappointment, resulting in late arrivals or, on occasion, no-shows.

At one point he looked over at me, smiled, then casually started singing "From a Jack to a King." He knew it was a favorite of mine. Later he sang "Do You Know Who I Am?" As I listened to the words, I couldn't help but relate to them.

After four years of lackluster songs, he was back on the charts again, and RCA could no longer complain about him. They'd been threatening the Colonel that if Elvis didn't have a recording session soon, they were going to rerelease some of his old songs.

One success led to another. Since his TV special, he was eager to begin performing in front of a live audience again, to prove to everyone that he hadn't lost his touch. Looking for the best source of immediate income, the Colonel made a deal with the nearly completed Las Vegas International for Elvis to headline there for a month, at a salary of half a million dollars.

Vegas was the challenge he needed to demonstrate that he could still captivate a live audience. This was what he loved most and did best. But it was a major challenge.

He hadn't made any real demands on his voice in years and now was locked into two shows a night for twenty-eight days straight. Anxious, he wondered whether he was up to the strain, whether he'd draw sell-out crowds, whether he would be able to hold an audience for a full two hours. He wanted this new act to be accepted, feeling he now had more than his rock-and-roll gyrations to offer.

Not only was this a crucial time in his career, but there was the additional pressure of the unprecedented fee and the fact that Las Vegas was the only city where he'd bombed, thirteen years earlier, in 1956.

He wasn't the kind of person who'd come out and say, "I'm scared." Instead I'd see it in his actions, his left leg shaking, and his foot tapping. He held in his fears and emotions until at times he would explode, tearing into anyone who happened to be around. At dinner one evening Elvis said that he was concerned about his hairstyle, and I mentioned I'd seen a billboard of Ricky Nelson on Sunset Boulevard. His hair was long with a slight wave, and I thought it was extremely appealing. I innocently suggested that Elvis take a look at it. "Are you goddamn crazy?" he shouted. "After all these years, Ricky Nelson, Fabian, that whole group have more or less followed in my footsteps, and now I'm supposed to copy them? You've gotta be out of your mind, woman."

He left the dinner table in a rage. He had always been hailed as an original and now he was afraid that in Vegas even that wouldn't be enough. I knew I had injured his ego and for that I apologized.

In preparing his show for the International, Elvis pulled out all the stops. He was in top form—on a natural high quite independent of pills. He was more trim and physically fit than he'd ever been.

Putting together the best musicians, sound and lighting technicians, costumers, and choreographers, he was taking no chances this time. He scoured the music scene for the top sidemen in the business. Auditions were held and he handpicked each player—names such as James

Burton, John Wilkinson, Ronny Tutt, Glen D. Hardin, Jerry Scheff. He loved the sound of the Sweet Inspirations, backup group for Aretha Franklin, and he hired them on the spot as a warmup act and to sing backup vocals. He also hired his favorite gospel group, the Imperial Quartet.

Before leaving Los Angeles, Elvis rehearsed at RCA Sound Studios for ten days and then polished the act for a full week prior to the opening. It was the event of the summer in Vegas. Colonel Parker brought the preopening publicity to fever pitch. Billboards were up all over town. On the third floor of the International, administrative offices bustled with activity. No other entertainer coming into Vegas had ever stimulated this kind of excitement. The hotel lobby was dominated by Elvis paraphernalia—pictures, posters, T-shirts, stuffed animals, balloons, records, souvenir programs. You'd think Barnum and Bailey were coming to town.

Back home there was also excitement as we girls discussed what we'd wear to the opening. "I want you to look extra special, Baby," Elvis said. "This is a big night for all of us." I hit every boutique in West L.A. before finding just the right outfit.

Though it had been nine years since Elvis had given a live performance, you never would have known it from his opening. The audience cheered the moment he stepped onstage and never stopped the entire two hours as Elvis sang, "All Shook Up," "Blue Suede Shoes," "In the Ghetto," "Tiger Man," and "Can't Help Falling in Love." He mixed the old with the new, the fast and hot with the lyrical and romantic. It was the first time I'd ever seen Elvis perform live. Wanting to surprise me, he had kept me from rehearsals. I was astounded. At the end he left them still cheering and begging for more.

Cary Grant was among the stars who came backstage to congratulate him after the show. But the most touching moment was when Colonel Parker arrived with tears in his eyes, wanting to know where his boy was. Elvis came out of the dressing room and the two men embraced. I believe everyone felt their emotion in that moment of triumph.

I don't think we slept that night. Joe Esposito brought in all the newspapers and we read the rave reviews declaring, "Elvis was great" and "He never looked or sang better." He shared credit for his new success with all of us.

"Well, we did it. It's going to be a long thirty days, but it's going to be worth it if we get the reception we got last night. I may have been a real tyrant, but it was well worth it."

"Yeah, you're right," we all agreed, laughing. "You were a tyrant."

The International Hotel was delirious over Elvis's performance and the box-office receipts. The following day they signed a five-year contract with the Colonel for Elvis to appear twice a year, usually around the same time, January and August, at the then unheard-of salary of one million dollars a year.

Elvis literally took over Las Vegas for the entire month he was there, playing to a packed house every show as thousands more were turned away. No matter where we looked, all we could see was the name ELVIS—

on television, newspapers, banners, and billboards. The King had returned.

Initially, Elvis's triumph in Las Vegas brought a new vitality to our marriage. He seemed a different person. Once again, he felt confident about himself as a performer and he continued to watch his weight and work out every day at karate.

It was also the first time that I felt we were functioning as a team. I made several trips to New York, trying to find unique accessories for him to wear onstage. I bought scarves, jewelry, and a black leather belt with chain links all around it that Bill Belew would later copy for the famous Elvis jumpsuit belts.

I loved seeing him healthy and happy again, and I especially enjoyed our early days in Vegas. The International provided an elegant three-bedroom suite that we turned into our home away from home. During his show I always sat at the same table down front, never tiring of watching him perform. He was spontaneous and one never knew what to expect from him.

On occasion, after his midnight show, we'd catch lounge acts of other performers playing Vegas or we'd gamble until dawn. Other times we'd relax backstage, visiting with entertainers captivated by his performance. This was the first time I'd been with Elvis at a high point in his career.

With the renewed fame came renewed dangers. Offstage he could be guarded by Sonny and Red. Onstage he was a walking target. One night that summer Joe and Sonny were tipped off that a woman in the audience was carrying a gun and had threatened to shoot Elvis. A true professional, Elvis insisted on going on. Additional precautions were taken and everyone was on the alert. Elvis was instructed to stay downstage, making himself a smaller target, and Sonny and Jerry were poised to jump in front of him at the slightest sign of suspicious movement in the audience. Red was positioned in the audience with the FBI agents.

The show seemed to take an eternity. I glanced at Patsy apprehensively and she in turn grasped my hand as we comforted each other, longing for the night to end without incident. Vernon remained backstage, never letting Elvis out of his sight and praying, "Dear God, don't let anything happen to my son."

Because of this and other threats, extra security was arranged wherever Elvis appeared. Entrances through backstages, kitchens, back elevators, and side exits became routine.

Elvis had his own theory about assassinations, based on the murders of the Reverend Martin Luther King, Jr., and Robert F. Kennedy. He felt that the assassins gloated over their "accomplishments," and told his bodyguards that if any attempt were made on his life, they should get the killer—even before the police. He didn't want anyone bragging to the media that they'd killed Elvis Presley.

Sonny and Red lived in so much tension these days that they were constantly frenzied. Suspicious in crowds of overzealous fans, they were quick to respond to any sign of danger. Compared to Sonny's diplomacy, Red's reputation was to act first and ask questions later. Eventually, numerous assault-and-battery charges started pil-

PRISCILLA BEAULIEU PRESLEY

ing up against Elvis. When Vernon warned him about
Sonny and Red's aggressiveness, Elvis said, "Goddamn,
Red. I hired you to keep the sons of bitches away from
me, not get me in any legal binds. Somehow you're
going to have to control that red-headed temper of yours."

Although Elvis would joke about the death threats—
and there would be several more throughout the Vegas
commitments—the fear and constant need for security
heightened the pressure of nightly performing.

In the beginning when Elvis began doing regular
Vegas engagements, we girls visited frequently. We'd fly
in over the weekend, sometimes bringing our children,
spend three or four days, and then return home.

On the days we were apart I'd take hundreds of Polar-
oids and home movies of Lisa. She was growing so rapidly I didn't want him to miss out on her development.
Daily he'd receive his "care packages," as I'd refer to
them, including tape recordings of me teaching Lisa new
words and Lisa mimicking me. Each week, upon my arrival, I'd paste photos on the mirrors in his bedroom to
remind him that he had a wife and child.

During his first couple of engagements he still seemed
humbled by lingering doubts of whether the public was
fully accepting him. At this point he had no interest in
outside affairs or flirtations, his concentration on daily
rehearsals and performances every evening excluding
everything else.

Later he would become more cocky. The crowds' admiration took him back to his triumphs in the early fif-
ties and he found it hard to come down to earth after a

276

month of nightly cheers. His name on the International's huge marquee would be replaced by the next superstar. The offices on the third floor would be cleared out and incoming calls for reservations would stop.

Thriving on all the excitement, glamour, and hysteria, he found it difficult to go home and resume his role as father and husband. And for me the impossibility of replacing the crowd's adoration became a real-life nightmare.

At home in Los Angeles, there was just the usual group around—strictly a family atmosphere. This abrupt change was too much for him and soon he developed the habit of lingering in Vegas for days, sometimes weeks, after a show. The boys were finding it increasingly difficult to resolve the conflict between working for Elvis and maintaining a home life.

Crazed with inactivity and boredom, Elvis became edgy and temperamental, a condition exacerbated by the Dexedrine he was again taking to control his weight.

Sometimes, to ease the transition home, Elvis would insist we all pile into cars and head for Palm Springs. Since our marriage we had spent many weekends there sunning and watching football games and late-night television, but after Lisa was born, my needs changed. The Palm Springs heat was too much for her, the long drive boring, the idleness of resort life wearying. One weekend I suggested, "Elvis, why don't just you and the guys go down?"

From that time on, the guys developed their own lifestyle in our secluded desert home. Occasionally we wives would be invited to spend the weekend, but by and large, Elvis now considered Palm Springs his private refuge.

He made it clear that this time away was good for him, giving him a chance to think, to hang out with the guys. In reality Elvis was lost. He did not know what to do with himself after Vegas. He escaped in more powerful, unnecessary prescribed drugs to raise his spirits and ward off boredom.

After he had conquered Vegas, it was agreed that Elvis should go back on the road. Colonel immediately began booking concert tours around the nation, starting with an impressive run of six sold-out shows in the Houston Astrodome, which earned over one million dollars in three nights.

The night I arrived in Texas to watch the performance, Joanie, Judy, and I flew in on a private jet. I looked down on the Astrodome and found it hard to believe my eyes. The length of a football field—and already sold out. It made *me* nervous. I could imagine how Elvis felt.

Elvis too found the Astrodome overwhelming. "Goddamn," he said when he first walked in. "They expect me to sell this son of a bitch out? It's a goddamn ocean."

However dwarfed he was by the giant facility, he electrified his audience. Houston was our first run-in with mass hysteria. The limousine was strategically parked by the stage door for Elvis's immediate getaway. Even so, screaming fans surrounded the car, frantically yelling out his name, presenting flowers, and trying to touch him.

If anything, Houston was an even greater victory than Vegas. The King of Rock and Roll was back on top. The strain of sustaining such a hype was just beginning and, for the moment, I could believe that everything would still be all right. I did not realize the extent to which Elvis's touring was going to separate us, that this in fact was the beginning of the end. After Houston Elvis began crossing the country, making one-night stands, flying by day, trying to catch some sleep to maintain the high energy level demanded by his performances. From 1971 on, he toured more than any other artist—three weeks at a time with no days off and two shows on Saturdays and Sundays.

I missed him. We talked constantly of being together more, but he knew that if he let me join him, he couldn't refuse the requests from regulars whose marriages were also feeling the strain of long separations. For a while a group of us would fly in from time to time, but this didn't last long. Elvis noticed that his employees were lax in discharging their duties to him when spouses were present, and he established a new policy: No wives on the road.

I didn't really miss the one-night stands, a tedious routine at best: Jump off the plane, rush to the hotel, unpack as little as possible, since you had to check out the next day, go to the performance, then back to the hotel for a little rest before heading back to the airport. Everything was the same except for the name of the town.

It was the day Elvis suggested I come to Vegas less often that I became really upset and suspicious. He'd decided that we wives would attend opening and closing nights only.

I knew then I'd have to fight for our relationship or accept the fact that we were now gradually going to grow apart as so many couples in show business do. As a couple, we'd never sat down to plan out a future. Elvis, individually, was stretching as an artist, but as man and wife we needed a common reality.

The chances of our marriage surviving were slim indeed as long as he continued to live apart from Lisa and me, and in bachelor quarters at that. It came down to how much longer I could stand the separation. Elvis wanted to have his cake and eat it too. And now, as the tours and long engagements took him even further from his family, I realized that we might never reach my dreams of togetherness. I had trouble believing that Elvis was always faithful, and the more he kept us apart, the more my suspicions grew.

Now when we went to Vegas, I felt more comfortable at the openings. He was always preoccupied with the show and I felt he needed me then. On closing nights I always felt uneasy. Too many days had gone by, enough time for suspicions to poison my thoughts. The Vegas maître d's invariably planted a bevy of beauties in the front rows for the entertainer to play to. Curious, I would scan their faces while watching Elvis closely to see if he seemed to direct his songs to any girl in particular. Suspicious of everyone, my heart ached—but we were never able to talk about it. It was to be accepted as part of the job.

Backstage one night Vernon was jokingly negotiating

for a key that had been tossed to Elvis. She was an attractive middle-aged blonde—Vernon's type. Elvis said, "Daddy, you've got enough problems at home with one blonde. You certainly don't need two."

"Well, okay," Vernon said. "You're going to have problems of your own if your wife goes out in the street looking like that." I had begun wearing skimpy knit dresses and see-through fabrics that were daringly revealing. Lamar and Charlie whistled and gave wolfcalls, while Elvis proudly showed me off.

The jokes I played on him were also efforts to get his attention. One night, after he'd left early for a show, I put on a black dress with a black hood and an exceptionally low-cut back. When it came time for Elvis to give away kisses to the girls in the audience—a regular part of his show—I went up to the stage. Instead of kissing me, he kept on singing his song, leaving me to stand there. With my hair hiding the dress strap around my neck, I appeared from the back to be nude from the waist up. I could hear the "oooh"s and "ahhhh"s of the audience. They were under the impression that a topless girl had cornered Elvis and that he couldn't figure out what to do.

I kept whispering to him, "Kiss me, kiss me, so I can sit down," but he decided to turn the joke on me, and made me wait in the spotlight for the duration of the song. Planting a big kiss on my lips, he surprisingly introduced me to the audience. I felt a bit embarrassed and made my way back to my seat.

Later in the show he'd strut back and forth onstage, tease his audience, talk to them, tell them stories, even confide in them. "You know," he'd say, "some people in this town get a little greedy. I know you folks save a long time to come and hear me sing. I just want you to know, as far as I'm concerned, there won't be any exorbitant raise in price when you come back. I'm here to entertain you and that's all I care about."

Elvis was having an ongoing love affair with his audience and the next time I was home alone I knew I had no choice but to start more of a life of my own.

It was with that thought in mind that Joanie, my sister Michelle, and I planned a short trip to Palm Springs. In the course of the weekend I opened the mailbox to check the mail and found a number of letters from girls who had obviously been to the house, one in particular signed "Lizard Tongue." My immediate response was disbelief, followed by outrage. I dialed Vegas and demanded that Joe find Elvis and bring him to the telephone. When Joe said Elvis was sleeping, I told him about the letters and insisted I speak to Elvis. Joe promised that he would have Elvis call as soon as he woke up. He did, but it was clear that Joe had filled him in on the situation and Elvis had his explanation ready. He was totally innocent, the girls were just fans, they were out of their minds if they said they'd ever come to the house, and besides, it was their word against his. As usual, in the end I apologized for putting him on the spot, but things at this point were becoming too obvious.

He said, "Get out and do things while I'm gone, because if you don't, you're going to start getting depressed."

Although my choices were limited—he still objected to my taking a job or enrolling in classes at college—I continued my dancing and started taking private art instruction.

Elvis was a born entertainer and although he tried to avoid crowds, disliked restaurants, and complained he "couldn't get out like a normal person," this life-style suited him. He handpicked the people he wanted to be around him—to work with and travel with—and they adjusted to his routine and his hours and his temperament. It was a pretty close clan throughout the years. A few arguments erupted and a few couples left over some misunderstandings, but they usually returned in a week or two.

My view of life had been fashioned by Elvis. I had entered his world as a young girl and he had provided absolute security. He distrusted any outside influences, which he saw as a threat to the relationship, fearing they would destroy his creation, his ideal. He could never have foreseen what was happening as the consequence of his prolonged absences from home. A major period in my growth was beginning. I still feared our separations but felt that our love had no boundaries, that I was his and if he wanted me to change, I would. For years nothing had existed in my world but him, and now that he was gone for long stretches of time, the inevitable happened. I was creating a life of my own, starting to achieve a sense of security in myself, and discovering there was a whole world outside our marriage.

Over the years of playing Vegas, other pressures began to mount. There were more death threats and lawsuits, including alleged paternity suits and assault-and-battery charges. Jealous husbands claimed they'd seen Elvis flirting with their wives, and others continued to charge that Sonny and Red were manhandling them. Elvis began to get bored with these nuisances as well as with the sameness of the show. Inevitably, he tried to change the format, but then he felt it just didn't have the same pacing as the original. He'd add a few songs here and there but then revert to the original. Pointed suggestions that he make changes before the next Vegas date added to the pressure.

Bored and restless, he increased his dependence on chemicals. He thought speed helped him escape from destructive thinking, when in reality it gave him false confidence and unnatural aggressiveness. He started losing perspective on himself and others. To me he became increasingly unreachable.

# 37

I HAD JUST walked into the living room where I found Elvis and Vernon arguing about Colonel Parker. "Goddamn, Daddy, call and tell him we're through. Tear up the goddamn contracts and I'll pay him whatever percentage we owe him."

"Listen, Son. Are you sure you want to do this?"

"Goddamn right I am. I hate what I'm doing and I'm goddamn bored."

Elvis stomped out the front door, never returning that evening nor the following few. We were mystified. For the first time he was traveling alone—without even one bodyguard. Elvis didn't even know his own phone number; nor did he carry cash. How was he going to get around? Arrangements had always been made for him.

According to Jerry Schilling, Elvis caught a commercial plane to Washington, D.C., with the intention of meeting President Nixon. When he arrived he had a sudden reaction to penicillin he had taken for a bad cold and decided to fly to L.A. He called during a stopover in Dallas, asking Jerry to meet him at LAX with a doctor. He wanted treatments for the reaction. Elvis rested two days in Los Angeles and then continued his journey back to Washington, D.C., along with Jerry and a five-hundred-dollar check that Jerry arranged to have cashed.

During the flight Elvis befriended a young soldier just returning from Vietnam. The soldier must have told him his life story. Before the plane landed Elvis asked Jerry for the five hundred dollars and handed it over to the young man, wishing him good luck. Jerry said, "Elvis, that's all we have." Elvis responded with, "Yeah, but he needs it worse than I do, Schilling."

Later in the flight, he asked the stewardess for a pen and some paper. Elvis was never much of a letter writer, but he now wrote President Nixon a letter explaining how he could assist the youth of today in getting off drugs. It was an impassioned plea, mistakes hastily scratched out and corrected as he poured out his thoughts.

Jerry arranged for a limo to pick them up at the airport and drive them to the White House. It was 6:30 A.M. and Elvis was dressed in black, including his black cape, sunglasses, his large gold International belt, and a cane. He approached the gate looking, as Jerry put it, like Dracula. His face was a bit swollen, and Jerry feared that his appearance would arouse suspicion.

As soon as Elvis explained who he was and that he had

a message for the President, he was promised the letter would be given to President Nixon by nine that morning. Elvis then had Jerry arrange for him to see John Finlator, Deputy Narcotics Director in Washington. Elvis truly wanted to help kids get off street drugs. Another purpose of Elvis's trip was to try to acquire a Federal Narcotics badge for himself.

Elvis was an avid badge collector. He had detective, police, and sheriff badges from all over the nation and the narc badge represented some kind of ultimate power to him. In Elvis's mind that badge would give him the right to carry any prescribed drug he had on his person. The badge would also give Elvis and his Memphis Mafia the right to carry arms. With the Federal Narcotics badge he could legally enter any country both wearing guns and carrying any drugs he wished.

His obsession with obtaining this badge was triggered by a private eye named John O'Grady whom Elvis had hired to handle a paternity suit. O'Grady showed Elvis his Federal Narc badge, and Elvis's mind started clicking immediately: How could he get one himself? John O'Grady mentioned that John Finlator was the man Elvis should see.

Elvis told Jerry to wait at the hotel in case the President called while Elvis himself went to see Finlator. Within an hour, Jerry received a call from Elvis, saying that his request had been denied by Finlator. Jerry was surprised at Elvis's emotional state. He sounded near tears when he said, "He won't let me have the badge." Jerry was able to lift his spirits by telling him he'd just received a call from the White House. "The President read your letter and wants to see you in twenty minutes."

Walking into the White House was no easy feat, even for Elvis Presley. The guards were friendly but cautious as they checked him out. Jerry too was searched before entering the Oval Office along with Sonny West, whom Jerry had called to join them. Sonny had been mystified by the call and was awestruck when he realized he was about to meet the President of the United States.

Elvis was led separately into the Oval Office. Jerry and Sonny were told they had to wait outside, though there was some slight chance they'd meet the President later. According to Jerry, they were brought into the Oval Office in less than a minute. Jerry knew that if there was a way to get them in, Elvis would do it, and he had come through. Not even the President was immune to his charm.

When Jerry and Sonny entered they saw that Elvis had made himself right at home. He introduced everyone and encouraged the President to give Jerry and Sonny cuff links, and was not shy in asking for mementos to take home to their wives. By the time he left the Oval Office he had added this most important badge to his collection. He emerged smiling, a different Elvis from the one who a few hours before was emotionally upset. Nixon overruled Finlator's decision and had the badge sent to the Oval Office, where he could present it to Elvis.

The argument about Colonel that started this escapade was never mentioned again.

# 38

OUR MARRIAGE WAS now part-time. He wanted freedom to come and go as he pleased—and he did. When he was home, he was attentive and loving as father and husband. But it was clearly understood that I was mainly responsible for the parenting of Lisa.

An incident occurred which made me realize that I needed to spend more time with Lisa. She, Elvis, and I were about to sit for a family portrait. I was dressing her while her nurse combed her hair. Then, as I started for the set, Lisa refused to go with me. "What's the matter?" I asked. "Come on, honey."

"No, no," she kept saying, hanging on to her nurse. When she started to cry, I got nervous and short-tempered, taking her by the hand and urging, as if a child could decipher my logic, "But you've *got* to be happy! You're going to take pictures with Mommy and Daddy."

Each shot was an effort as we tried to coax her to laugh. For a moment we would be successful but then tears would reappear. She even cried sitting on her daddy's lap as I bribed her with toys and little dolls to get a smile.

That's when it hit me. My God, she's so attached to the nurse that she doesn't want to leave her. Now I knew I had to find more time to be with her. She had been affected by my own predicament. Busy centering my life around Elvis, even during his absences, I had neglected not only my needs but my daughter's as well.

I was torn between the two of them. When he was home I wanted to be with him, without other responsibilities, but I also wanted to be with Lisa, knowing how much she needed me.

I began taking Lisa to parks, afternoon parties, and daily swimming lessons at the YWCA, and I convinced myself that soon I'd no longer have to fake it with toys and lollipops and ice cream cones to get her to smile at me.

She would sit between Elvis and me at the dinner table, squeezing spinach through her hands and smearing it on her face. Elvis tried to convince himself that he found all this adorable, but the fact of the matter was that he was finicky about his food. With a good-natured laugh he would excuse himself, telling the maid, "We'll be eating in the den. Lisa will join us after she's finished playing with her meal."

When Elvis was away from home, which unfortunately was most of the time in those days, I continued to dispatch my regular care packages full of pictures and home movies documenting every inch of Lisa's growth. When he was with us, I encouraged him to participate in Easter-egg hunts and other outings, inviting Joe, Joanie, their children, and other family friends to join us.

Lisa and I visited him in Vegas for her birthdays, having huge parties in the suite, where she received everything from slot machines to two Saint Bernard puppies (a gift of Colonel Parker's) to an entire room filled with balloons—everything, in short, a two- or three-year-old shouldn't have and couldn't appreciate.

It was important to me that Elvis be home for Mother's Day and Father's Day, but he'd invariably call and say he couldn't make it, then try to compensate by bringing home extravagant gifts like a marble jewel box filled with diamond rings, necklaces, and earrings, or a whole wardrobe of handpicked designer clothes from a boutique in Vegas. But that wasn't the point. I didn't want the furs and jewels—I had all I could possibly use—I just wanted him home. It was a constant effort, single-handedly trying to keep up family traditions.

Although Elvis much preferred to spoil Lisa, he did discipline her from time to time. Once he paddled her for writing all over a beautiful velvet couch with crayons. Then he immediately went into a panic, wanting me to assure him that he'd done the right thing and that Lisa wouldn't hold it against him. When I told him, "If you hadn't spanked her, I'd have," he felt better. The only other time he touched her in anger was after we'd repeatedly warned her not to go near the pool and she did.

(She remembers this well and is proudly pleased by her two paddlings.)

By the time Lisa was four, she realized she could manipulate the help. Whenever one of them refused to do something for her, she'd threaten, "I'm gonna tell my daddy and you're going to get fired." Since none of them wanted her going to Elvis, they'd let her get her way, from staying up until all hours and skipping nightly baths to staying home from school. The result was that Lisa had trouble learning what was right and wrong and what she could and couldn't do.

"You don't treat people that way," I told her. "It's abusive. Yes, they work for your father. But you don't go around threatening them." Used to seeing people jump at her father's command, Lisa took years to overcome this habit. At family gatherings today with Jerry Schilling, Joe Esposito, and Dee Presley's sons Ricky and David, we still joke about Lisa's imperious past.

Since Elvis had started performing again, our home on Hillcrest had become so public that we could scarcely get in and out of the drive. Photographers actually concealed themselves in our backyard, making their presence known at the most inopportune moments. Once, we were relaxing at the pool, sunbathing, when I leaned over and gave Elvis a lingering kiss. He whispered, "What's that noise? Shhh, be quiet. Sonny! Jerry! It's a goddamn camera clicking off!" Elvis jumped up and they all headed after the poor man, Elvis leading, shouting obscenities and threats. This was one member of the press who I'm sure never returned.

In our three years on Hillcrest, we'd gradually outgrown the house. Lisa and her nurse shared one room, Charlie had the other, and Patsy and Gee and their new baby occupied the cottage out back. Elvis felt we needed more room; he wanted Sonny on call and close by. Discussions about a new home took on a new urgency.

When a couple of old regulars, broke and jobless, showed up at our door, Elvis took pity on them and put them up in our living room. I awoke in the early morning to the sound of blaring music and found the two had passed out from drinking Jack Daniel's and Coke. Half-empty glasses were strewn about the room and ashes littered the carpet. I felt my home was being turned into a boarding house.

"They have no respect for anything," I complained to Elvis later that day. "What if they fall asleep with cigarettes in their hands? We'll all go up in flames. How long do you intend for them to stay?" I was making no secret of my disapproval. "I don't want Lisa around this."

"You're right, Honey. Maybe I'll just head out for Palm Springs tonight."

The search for a new home led us to Holmby Hills, an exclusive area of sprawling estates between Bel Air and Beverly Hills. We found a traditional two-story house, well-situated on a hill, surrounded by two acres of well-manicured lawns and orange groves. It was larger than our other Los Angeles homes, with a high fence and forbidding gates to assure our privacy.

I had hoped that this home would redirect his attention to the family and that his weekends away in Palm Springs would now be spent with us. He had his own office, his own den, his own game room, his own theater, a breakfast room for private meals, and a dining room for family and friends. It was my intention to decorate this home exclusively to his liking, with ideas carried over from the Hillcrest house, which had been his favorite.

The house cost around $335,000, a little over the budget that we had in mind. With some persistence on our part, Vernon warily let me hire a professional to help furnish it. This would be the first house I'd decorated from scratch and I found it tremendously exciting—having plans drawn up, choosing color schemes, fabrics, wall coverings, and antiques. I loved hunting for special pieces of furniture: a china cabinet that concealed a television set, old trunks to be used as coffee tables, and antique vases to convert into lamps. I was so excited with the project that I persuaded Elvis not to look at the preliminary stages and to wait until everything was completed. Decorating became my passion. I found the challenge so absorbing that I was able to forget my worries over our relationship. Instead of pondering my loneliness, I was engaged in constructive work that required all the flair, imagination, and organizational ability I could summon.

At this time another fulfilling and liberating force entered my life—karate. It had been Elvis's love and hobby for years, and when I first took it up, it was just another of my efforts to get his attention and approval, as in the past when I'd enrolled in French classes because he liked the language, took flamenco dancing because he was an aficionado, and ballet because he adored dancers' bodies.

He had long admired kung fu expert Ed Parker, whom

he'd met years ago. I began taking private lessons under Ed's guidance three times a week. I soon learned there was much more to this art than violence. It was a philosophy. I became even more involved when Elvis cheered my progress.

On our return to Memphis, he slept throughout the day and I enrolled in another oriental discipline, the Korean art of Tae Kwan Do. I became as obsessive as Elvis in dedicating myself to this art. A mandatory requirement was memorizing forms, katas, and stances in the Korean language as well as learning the history of Tae Kwan Do.

The training was incredibly exacting. Over and over we'd execute the same movement until perfected. Perspiration poured into my eyes and yet, if I wiped it away, it would mean one hundred pushups under the watchful eyes of the entire classroom, a humiliation I did not desire and managed to avoid.

Now I could understand Elvis's enslavement to karate. It was an accomplishment, an achievement of confidence and physical mastery of self. In 1972, while Elvis was performing in Vegas, I met one of the top karate experts in the United States at the time, Mike Stone. On this particular evening he was acting bodyguard to a prominent record producer. After the show they came to visit Elvis backstage. Everyone was more impressed with Stone than with the boisterous tycoon he was protecting. Elvis was complimentary and he, Sonny, and Red had numerous questions. Several years earlier we had watched Stone at a tournament in Hawaii and we'd admired his fighting technique.

Later that evening, up in the Imperial Suite, Elvis encouraged me to train with Mike. "He has that killer quality. Nothing on two legs can beat him. I've been impressed with him since the first time I saw him fight. He's a real badass—I like the cat's style."

Back in Los Angeles I made arrangements with Mike to drive out to his studio later in the week and sit in on one of his classes. It was a long forty-five-minute drive.

Elvis was right. Mike exuded confidence and style, as well as a good deal of personal charm and wit. A deep friendship would develop. Because of the distance, I decided to continue my training with a friend of his, Chuck Norris, who had a studio closer to my home. Mike would sometimes come to Chuck's studio as a guest trainer.

I was emerging from Elvis's closed world, becoming aware of how sheltered my existence had been. Mike and Chuck introduced me to popular Japanese martial-arts films such as the Blind Swordsman series, and with Mike I attended karate tournaments locally and in neighboring counties, taking home movies and still photos of top karate fighters. I wanted to capture their individual styles so I could share them with Elvis, hoping this was something we could enjoy in common. In the end, though, I made a whole new circle of friends with whom I felt accepted for myself. The martial arts gave me such confidence and assurance that I began to experience my feelings and express my emotions as never before. Accustomed to suppressing my anger, I could honestly vent it now without the fear of accusations or explosions. I stopped apologizing for my opinions and laughing at jokes I didn't find amusing. A transformation had begun in which fear and indifference had no place. Along with this new confidence, off came my false eyelashes and heavy makeup, the jewels and flashy clothes. All devices that I'd depended upon for security I now shed.

I was seeing myself for the first time, and it was going to take a while for me to get used to the image. I had a chance to observe marriages outside our immediate circle, where the woman had just as much say as a man in everyday decisions and long-term goals. I was confronted with the harsh realization that living the way I had for so long was very unnatural and detrimental to my well-being. My relationship with Mike had now developed into an affair.

I still loved Elvis greatly, but over the next few months I knew I would have to make a crucial decision regarding my destiny. I knew that I must take control of my life. I could not give up these new insights. There was a whole world out there and I had to find my own place in it.

I wished that there was some way for me to share my experience and growth with Elvis. From my adolescence, he had fashioned me into the instrument of his will. I lovingly yielded to his influence, trying to satisfy his every desire. And now he wasn't here.

Accustomed to living in dark rooms, hardly seeing the sun, depending on chemical aids for sleep and wakefulness, surrounded by bodyguards who distanced us from reality, I yearned for the more ordinary pleasures. I began to appreciate the simple things that I would have liked to share with Elvis and hadn't: walks in the park, a candlelight dinner for two, laughter.

Elvis must have perceived my new restlessness. A couple of months later in Las Vegas, Joanie, Nora Fike, Red's wife Pat, and I were having dinner in the Italian restaurant at the Hilton between Elvis's shows. The maître d' came to the table with a message that Elvis wanted to see me upstairs in the suite. I remember thinking how unusual this was. Elvis rarely went to the suite between shows.

I went upstairs, filled with curiosity, and when I arrived in the suite I found Elvis lying in bed, obviously waiting for me. He grabbed me and forcefully made love to me. It was uncomfortable and unlike any other time he'd ever made love to me before, and he explained, "This is how a real man makes love to his woman." This was not the gentle, understanding man that I grew to love. He was under the influence, and with my personal growth and new realities he had become a stranger to me.

I wept in silence as Elvis got up to dress for the show. In order for our marriage to survive, Elvis would have had to take down all the artificial barriers restricting our life as a couple. There was too much room for doubt, too many unanswered questions for the mind to play upon. It was difficult for him to come to terms with his role as father and husband. And since neither of us had the ability to sit down and squarely face the issues jeopardizing the family, there seemed to be no hope.

What really hurt was that he was not sensitive to me as a woman and his attempt at a reconciliation had come too late; I had taken possession of my life.

That night I didn't close my eyes at all, grieving over

what I had to tell him. This was my one great love. Looking down at him I thought of all the times I'd traced my fingers over his lips, his nose, brushed my fingers through his hair, always while he slept. And now, I waited for him to wake up, waited for the right moment, if there ever could be one. At this point in our marriage we were so seldom together that I was having difficulty envisaging his reaction to my news; it had seemed so much easier to play it out in my imagination.

It was shortly after 2 P.M. I had already gotten up and started packing my things when Elvis awoke fairly alert and asked, "Where are you going?"

"I have to go back."

"So soon? It's early. You usually don't go back this early."

"I know," I agreed. "But I have to get back. I have things to do." I hesitated. "But first I have to tell you something." I stopped packing and looked at him. "This is probably the most difficult thing I'm ever going to have to say." I took a long pause, hardly able to get the words out. "I'm leaving."

Elvis sat up and asked. "What do you mean, leaving?"

Never in the entire time of our marriage had I ever suggested walking out on him.

"I mean our marriage."

"Are you out of your mind? You have everything any woman could want. You can't mean that, Sattnin. God-damn," he said, his voice filled with anguish. "I don't believe what I'm hearing. You mean I've been so blind that I didn't know what's going on? I've been so wrapped up I didn't see this coming."

"We're living separate lives."

Finally he asked, "Have I lost you to another man?"

"It's not that you've lost me to another man, you've lost me to a life of my own. I'm finding myself for the first time."

He looked up and stared at me in silence as I stood packing and snapped my suitcase shut. I tried to walk to the door but couldn't stop myself from running back into his arms. We hugged, tears streaming down our faces. "I have to go," I said. "If I stay now I'll never leave." I broke away, grabbed my suitcase, and headed for the door.

"Cilla," Elvis called. I stopped dead in my tracks. "Maybe another time, another place," he said slowly.

"Maybe so," I replied, looking back. "This just isn't the time."

And I walked out the door.

My trip to Memphis was unexpected and brief and there was only one purpose—to get my belongings. I wanted to spend as little time as possible there. Graceland had been my home, and it was difficult saying goodbye to everyone. The staff, most of whom I'd hired, seemed to know without my telling them that I was leaving for good. No one said a word, but their tearful hugs spoke volumes.

I found Dodger in her room—now downstairs—and

sat at her feet as she rocked in her chair. "Oh no," she said, "don't tell me that, Honey. You don't mean it." Then, realizing I did mean it, she hastened to ask, "You're gonna call me, aren't you, and keep in touch?"

"Yes, Dodger. I'll always be there for you. I'll come back and visit. We'll talk just like we always have, and nothing will ever change."

"You're like my own," Dodger said. "It's not going to be the same here without you. Poor little things. I feel so sorry for both of you."

Grandma wept as she tried to understand why two people who love each other should part. "I tried to tell him to spend more time with you—you and that baby."

"It's nobody's fault, Grandma. It's just life. We still love each other. We always will."

"I believe you'll get back together again, Hon." She was wringing her hands. "God knows, you two young'uns love each other enough."

There was a view of green pastures beyond Grandma's window—Sun, the old barn, and all the memories that went along with the happiest time of our lives. Thank God it was a beautiful day; I always hated rainy days at Graceland—they reminded me of the lonely winters when he was gone.

In the warmth and sunshine outside, I strolled around the grounds, looking one last time at the front porch where Elvis and I had sat on the steps, dreaming of a European trip that would have taken us back to Goethestrasse, where we'd met. Gazing over the lawns and the long circular driveway toward the Music Gates, where the fans always waited, I wondered if I'd ever return. I made my way back between the little craters left over from fireworks wars, and, in the garage, ran my hand over the shiny surface of a go-cart. I couldn't believe it was over.

# 39

LIKE MOST COUPLES breaking up, we went through a rough period before we finally accepted the fact that we were separating. We were divorced on October 9, 1973. Although Elvis and I had continued to talk regularly, we hadn't seen each other over the past few months, which had been a period of strain and tension as attorneys attempted to work out details. Eventually Elvis and I resolved them ourselves. We were both sensitive enough and still caring enough of each other's feelings to know that we wanted to avoid bitter accusations and futile attempts to assign blame. Our principal concern was Lisa, whose custody we agreed would be mutually shared. We remained so close that Elvis never bothered to pick up his copy of the divorce papers.

Accompanied by my sister Michelle, I waited in the

courthouse in Santa Monica, California, for him to arrive, and when he did, I was shocked by his appearance. His hands and face were swollen and puffy and he was perspiring profusely.

With Vernon and Michelle and our attorneys following, we went into the judge's chambers. Elvis and I sat before the judge and held hands as he put us through the formalities of the divorce proceedings. I hardly heard a word, I was bewildered by Elvis's physical condition and kept running my fingers back and forth across his swollen hands.

I wondered whether Elvis's new girlfriend, Linda Thompson, knew how much love and attention he needed. "Sattnin," I whispered, "is she takin' good care of you—watchin' your weight and your diet, waits for you to fall asleep at night?"

Then the judge was finished. The dream I had had of a perfect union was over. The hope of an ideal marriage, which had consumed all my thoughts and energy since I was fourteen, had ended with the simple stroke of a pen.

Feeling a great sense of emptiness, I walked with Michelle to my car. Elvis, his father, his attorney, and a few of the guys walked over to his limo. In passing I waved, he winked. The affinity we shared for each other would always be there. We continued to talk frequently, particularly about Lisa, who we knew would be unhappy. We wanted her to know that she would not, in any way, be deprived of either of us. When we were together it was as if we'd never parted, exchanging loving kisses and sitting arm in arm with her in our laps, and, when we were apart, we never criticized each other.

She'd visit Elvis often in both L.A. and Memphis. He assured me that he would take good care of her, but his life-style was such that I could not help worrying. I'd call to check on her nearly every night she was away. It was 1 A.M. in Memphis when I asked Elvis, "Did Lisa have her bath, and is she in bed yet?"

"Yeah, she's taken care of," he said. "She's in bed, fast asleep."

Within minutes, Aunt Delta called me and complained that Lisa wasn't in bed and she couldn't get her to take her bath. I talked to Lisa, who said, "Well, Daddy wanted me to stay up."

When I called Elvis back, I said, "I thought you told me she was in bed."

"Ah, let her stay up," he said. "It's no big deal."

Her daddy handed everything over to her on the proverbial silver platter, which created conflict when she'd come home and have to deal with reality. We had a running debate on how she was to be raised. "To hell with values," Elvis would say, joking. I knew that it was essential that Lisa gain some perspective, but try to explain that to Elvis Presley.

As the months passed, Linda Thompson became his constant companion and was good for him, I felt. He began taking trips to Aspen and Hawaii, getting out more, because of Linda's outgoing personality. When we spoke, he seemed to be in good spirits.

His movie career was at a standstill, and he focused on Vegas appearances and touring. Elvis had trouble seeing himself "a forty-year-old man still shaking to 'Hound Dog.'" He had other ambitions. He once talked of producing, even directing, but he never took steps to pursue either.

Then came an offer. Barbra Streisand and Jon Peters approached him to star opposite Barbra in a remake of *A Star Is Born*. When Elvis called me from Vegas, I got the impression he was going to do it. His energy and enthusiasm were electric. It was a film classic and he saw a chance to make a breakthrough into dramatic roles. He was confident he could play Norman Mayne.

"It looks like a sure thing," he said. "Just the details have to be worked out." But the project ran aground on those details. It was Jon Peters's first movie. That he was to direct this film with no credits, no track record, presented a problem in Colonel Parker's estimation. Another difficulty was the fact that Elvis's billing would be second to Barbra's—something the Colonel wouldn't hear of. The project was rejected, leaving Elvis despondent over the lost opportunity.

In time, it became evident that he was letting his health go. His behavior at times was deliberately self-destructive. On a few occasions he'd say, "I'll never make it much beyond forty." We've all made such statements, but with Elvis the thought was deep-seated and chronic. Gladys had died at forty-two and, like Gladys, he wanted to go before his father, sensing that he himself couldn't bear another loss.

From time to time, I'd hear that he had checked into the hospital. Concerned, I'd call, asking, "Are you all right?"

"Sure," he'd say, laughing a little to show me it was all a big joke. "Nungen needs a little rest, Sattnin." Then I realized he'd gone to the hospital for the same reason he had during his Army days. It was his way of taking a little rest; he needed to get out of Graceland and away from all the pressures.

By 1976 everyone was becoming alarmed over his mental state as well as his physical appearance. His face was bloated, his body unnaturally heavy. The more people tried to talk to him about this, the more insistent he became that everything was all right.

The Colonel was even concerned about Elvis's actions while onstage. Elvis started forgetting lyrics and resorting to sheet music. He was acting erratic by ignoring the audience and playing to the band. A few shows were canceled and no one could predict whether or not he'd appear onstage.

In the absence of any significant professional challenge, Elvis created his own real-life dramas. His fascination with guns was now an obsession. He became paranoid over death threats, and from his association with the Memphis local police, he had access to lists of local drug pushers. He felt he personally should get them off the streets. Phoning me late one evening, he said, "Cilla, you have anyone you want taken care of? Strictly top secret."

The style, grace, and pride that for the past eight years had been the hallmark of a Presley live performance now bordered on self-parody. Frustrated with the lack of challenge of each passing show, Elvis resorted to sheer flamboyance, symbolized by his costumes, each more elaborate than the one before, loaded with an overabundance of fake stones, studs, and fringes. There were voluminous capes and cumbersome belts to match. He was performing in garb that added thirty-five pounds to his weight. It was as if he were determined to upstage himself instead of relying on his raw talent.

There were times in his final year that he would be criticized on how he related to his audience. Some people observed that he joked around with his band too much and left his songs unfinished. Once Elvis even complained from the stage about "bad management" at the hotel, citing a certain employee at the Hilton who was being fired. The following day Colonel Parker asked Elvis to stick to his own business—entertaining—and let the hotel handle its help. Vernon tended to take Elvis's side on this as on every issue, but the Colonel had a right to be concerned.

One of the guys actually told Elvis he was beginning to look more like a Liberace act in the hope that Elvis would take the hint and come to his senses and rely on just his talent. But from the beginning Elvis had insisted: "I just want to read positive reviews. I don't want to hear any negativity." As a teenager he'd been shielded by Gladys from criticism. When she'd filled her albums and scrapbooks, she'd used only the favorable clippings. If he hadn't been so sheltered, he might have had a better perspective on his career. At least he'd have been aware of what was being written about him and possibly used some of the comments constructively.

No matter what he did, his fans still cheered him on. They were faithful to him through good performances and bad, and eventually their love was the only real gratification he received. They endorsed everything he did. Maybe as long as he was getting their cheers, he thought he was doing fine. But in fact Colonel Parker was right when he told Elvis that he'd better get himself straightened out or his whole career would go down the drain.

His personal life was not helping the situation. He was seeing Ginger Alden, who was twenty years his junior, and the difference in their ages was becoming more and more of a problem. He'd say, "I'm tired of raising kids. I don't have the patience to go through it all over again." There were conflicts—many. Ginger did not like touring, one-night stands. She was close to her family and didn't want to leave them. Elvis tried bringing half her family with them, but that only created other problems. "She spends more time with her sister and mother than she does with me," he complained.

In discussing his dilemma, I asked, "Do you think you can really live with just one woman?"

"Yes," he answered. "Now more than ever. I know I've done some stupid things, but the stupidest was not realizing what I had until I lost it. I want my family back."

I wondered if there was some way we could make it work. "Maybe it was just too early in life for us, Sattnin," I said. "Maybe one day there will be a time for us."

"Yeah," Elvis laughed. "When I'm seventy and you're sixty. We'll both be so old we'll look really silly, racing around in golf carts."

In April 1977 Elvis fell ill and had to cancel his tour and return home to Graceland. Lisa and I were there visiting Dodger. He called me up to his room. He did not look himself; his face and body were bloated. He was wearing pajamas, which he seemed to prefer these days when at home. He held Cheiro's *Book of Numbers* and told me there was something he wanted me to read. His curiosity for answers had not abated. He was still searching for his purpose in life, still feeling he had not found his calling. If he had found a cause to espouse, whether a drugless society or world peace, he would have had the role he sought in life. His generosity was evidence of this part of his nature—his legendary penchant for giving, even to the countless people he didn't know.

But he never found a crusade to pull him out of his cloistered world, a discipline strong enough to counter his escape into drugs. That night he read to me, searching for answers, just as he had done the year before and the year before that and the years before that.

# 40

WE BOARDED the *Lisa Marie* around nine o'clock that evening, just my parents, Michelle, Jerry Schilling, Joan Esposito, and a few close friends. At first, I just sat alone, in despair. Then I went to the back of the plane, to Elvis's bedroom. I lay there, unable to believe that Elvis was really dead.

I remembered the jokes Elvis used to make about dying. He'd say, "It'd really take something for me to leave this earth." Yet he wore a chain around his neck that had both a cross and a Star of David on it. He would joke about it, saying he wanted to be covered in all areas, just in case.

He'd had a fear of flying, but he never showed it. Elvis never showed any of his fears. He felt he had a responsibility to make everyone else feel secure. So he gave the impression he was self-assured, because he didn't want to let any of us down.

I thought of a time when we were on a flight home from Los Angeles. There was a lot of turbulence, and the plane was shaking badly. Everyone on board was frightened. Everyone but Elvis. When I looked at him, he was smiling, and then he took my hand. "Don't worry," he said. "We're gonna make it." Suddenly, I felt safe. There was a certainty about Elvis. If he said it was going to be, then it was going to be that way.

The trip seemed endless. By the time we reached Memphis, I was numb. We were ushered into a waiting limousine, to avoid the crush of photographers. Then we sped off to Graceland, where we were met by frantic, disbelieving faces: relatives and close friends, the maids—the same people who had been around us for so many years. I had spent most of my life with these people and seeing them now was devastating.

Most of Elvis's close family—Vernon, Grandma, her daughters, Delta and Nash, and others—congregated in Grandma's room, while his friends, and the guys who worked for him, were mostly gathered in the den. Everyone else seemed to just be walking in and out of the rooms, silent and solemn, glancing around in disbelief.

Lisa was outside on the lawn, with a friend, riding around on the golf cart that her father had given her. At first I was amazed that she was able to play at a time like this, but when I talked to her, I realized that the full impact of what happened hadn't hit her yet. She'd seen the paramedics rushing Elvis away, and he was still at the hospital when I'd arrived, so Lisa was confused.

"Is it true?" she asked. "Is my daddy really gone?"

Again, I was really at a loss for words. She was our child. It was difficult enough for me to believe and confront Elvis's death myself. I just didn't know how to tell her that she would never see her daddy again.

I nodded, then took her into my arms. We hugged and then she ran out and started riding around in her golf cart again. But now I was glad she could play. I knew it was her way of avoiding reality.

The night seemed endless. Several of us sat around the dining room table talking, and it was then that I learned the circumstances of Elvis's death. I was told that Elvis had played racquetball with his cousin, Billy Smith, until four o'clock that morning, while Billy's wife, Jo, and Elvis's girlfriend, Ginger, watched them. Then they all presumably retired for the night. But as Ginger slept, Elvis stayed up to read. He called down to his Aunt Delta for some ice water and said he was having a hard time sleeping.

Elvis was still reading when Ginger woke up at nine o'clock that morning, and then she went back to sleep until about 1 P.M. When she awoke, Elvis was not in bed. She found him lying face down on his bathroom floor.

Ginger called downstairs, and Al Strada and Joe Esposito came running up. After calling the paramedics, Joe gave Elvis mouth-to-mouth resuscitation until they arrived. As the paramedics were leaving to rush Elvis to the hospital, his personal physican, "Dr. Nick," arrived and rode in the ambulance, working on Elvis all the way to Baptist Memorial. There the staff tried for another half an hour to revive Elvis, but it was all futile. He was pronounced dead on arrival of heart failure. Vernon then requested an autopsy. The body was taken to the Memphis Funeral Home to be prepared for viewing in Graceland the following day.

As I sat listening to the events leading up to Elvis's last hours, I became more and more disturbed. There were so many questions. Elvis was seldom left alone for any length of time.

Suddenly I knew I had to be alone. I went upstairs to Elvis's private suite, where we had spent so much of our life together. The rooms were more orderly than I'd expected. Many of his personal belongings were gone; his nightstand was bare of books.

I went into his dressing room and it was as if I could sense his living presence—his own unique scent filled the room. It was an eerie sensation.

From the dining room window I could see thousands of people out on Elvis Presley Boulevard waiting for the hearse that would bring his body back to Graceland. His music filled the air as radio stations throughout the nation paid tribute to the King.

Soon the casket was placed in the entrance hall and opened for viewing. I sat in Grandma's room most of that afternoon as thousands of mourners from all over the world passed by, paying their last respects. Many wept; some men and women even fainted. Others lingered at the casket, refusing to believe it was him. He was truly loved, admired, and respected.

I waited for the right moment for Lisa and me to say goodbye. It was late that evening, and Elvis had already been moved to the living room where the funeral was to be held. It was quiet; everyone had left. Together we stood over him, emotional. "You look so peaceful, Satt-nin, so rested. I know you'll find happiness and all the answers there." Then I joked, "Just don't cause any trouble at the Pearly Gates." Lisa took my hand and we placed a sterling silver bracelet depicting a mother and child's clasped hands on his right wrist. "We'll miss you." I knew my life would never be the same.

Colonel came to the funeral wearing his usual baseball hat, shirt, and slacks. He disguised his emotions as best he could. Elvis had been like his own son. From the old school, the Colonel was considered a coldhearted busi-nessman, but in truth he had stayed faithful and loyal to Elvis, even when his career began to slip. This day he asked Vernon to sign a contract extending his position as Elvis's manager. He was already planning ways to keep Elvis's name before the public. He acted quickly, fearful that with Elvis gone, Vernon would be too distraught to handle correctly the many proposals and propositions that would be in the offing. Vernon signed.

At the service, Lisa and I sat with Vernon and his new fiancée, Sandy Miller, Dodger, Delta, Patsy, my parents, Michelle, and the rest of the family. George Hamilton was there. Ann-Margret attended with her husband, Roger Smith. Ann expressed her sympathy so sincerely I felt a genuine bond with her.

J.D. and the Stamps Quartet sang Elvis's favorite gos-pel songs. Vernon had chosen the preacher, a man who hardly knew Elvis and spoke mostly of his generosity.

Elvis would probably have laughed and told his daddy, "Couldn't you have got a comedian or something?" Elvis would not have wanted us to grieve.

After the service we drove to the cemetery, Lisa and I riding with Vernon and Sandy. It was three miles away and for the whole three miles both sides of the street were lined with mourners, and at the cemetery there were thousands more. The pallbearers—Jerry Schilling, Joe Esposito, George Klein, Lamar Fike, Billy Smith, Charlie Hodge, Dr. Nick, and Gene Smith—carried the casket to the marble mausoleum where Elvis was finally laid to rest. There we held a short ceremony and, one by one, walked to the coffin, kissed or touched it, and spoke a few words of farewell. Shortly after, for security reasons, he was moved to Graceland in the meditation garden, his final resting place.

Before Lisa and I returned to L.A., Vernon called me to his office. He was overwhelmed with grief. Did I know anything that would help him to understand why his son had died? He never fully accepted it, and I believed his pain led to his own death, just as Grandma later never recovered from Vernon's death.

When Lisa and I returned home I was torn, trying to decide what was best for her. Many conflicting stories were coming out in the national publications and I knew these could have a lasting negative effect on her memory of her father. I decided to send her to summer camp. There she could be protected from radio, TV, and newspapers and could be with her many friends, including Debbie and Cindy, Joe and Joanie's children.

By the time she returned, I'd already made plans with

Michelle for a long trip to Europe. Anything to get away from the constant reminders that filled the media.

Elvis's death made me much more aware of my own mortality and that of the people I loved. I realized I'd better start sharing a lot more with the people that I cared about, and every moment that I had with my child or my parents became more precious.

I learned from Elvis, often—sadly—from his mistakes. I learned that having too many people around can sap your energies. I learned the price of trying to make everyone happy. Elvis would bestow gifts on some, making others jealous, often creating rivalries and anxieties within the group. I learned to confront people, and to face issues—two steps Elvis had avoided.

I learned to take charge of my life. Elvis had been so young when he became a star that he was never able to handle the power and money that accompanied his fame. In many ways, he was a victim, destroyed by the very people who catered to his every want and need. He was a victim, too, of his image. His public wanted him to be perfect while the press mercilessly exaggerated his faults. He never had the chance to be human, to grow up to be a mature adult, to experience the world outside his artificial cocoon.

When Elvis Presley died, a little of our own lives was taken from each of us who knew and loved Elvis Presley, who shared in his music, his films, who followed his career. His passion was entertaining his friends and fans. His audience was his true love. And the love Elvis and I shared was a deep and abiding one.

He was, and remains, the greatest influence in my life.

# Epilogue

I HAVE SPENT countless hours recalling moments in my past that are to me somewhat significant, memorable pieces of history. When I first decided to tell this story, I had no idea what a difficult and emotional task it would be. So much has been said and written about Elvis from those who knew him well to those who did not and said they did. I hoped to give a better perception of what he was as a man. Other books have painted a picture rather less than flattering, harboring on weaknesses, eccentricities, violent temper tantrums, perversions, and drug abuse. I wanted to write about love and precious, wonderful moments and ones filled with grief and disappointments, about a man's truimphs and defeats, much of it with a child-woman at his side, feeling and experiencing his pain and joys as if they were one.

I would not be honest if I did not say revealing our life, which was so dearly coveted, has been more than a struggle for me. There were many times I wanted to back out, give up, forget or not deal with this labor of love. Some will find I have left out many important dates, specific facts, and countless stories. I don't think anyone can begin to capture the magic, sensitivity, vulnerability, charm, generosity, and greatness of this man who influenced and contributed so much to our culture through his art and music. I did not intend to accomplish such a feat, just to tell a story. Elvis was a giving soul who touched and gave happiness to millions all over the world and continues to be respected and loved by his peers.

He was a man, a very special man.